Teachings From The Bhagavad Gita For The Householder Yogi

In The Light Of Kriya Yoga

Rudra Shivananda

Alight Publications

2023

Teachings From The Bhagavad Gita For The Householder Yogi

By Rudra Shivananda

First Edition Published in December 2023

Alight Publications
PO Box 277
Live Oak, CA 95953
email: alightpub@gmail.com

Teachings From The Bhagavad Gita For the Householder Yogi © 2023 by Runbir Singh.

All rights reserved. No part of this publication may be reproduced, stored in a retrieval system or database, or transmitted in any form or by any means electronic, mechanical, photocopying, recording, or otherwise without the prior written approval of the author or publisher.

Softback ISBN: 978-1-931833-66-4

Hardcover ISBN: 978-1-931833-65-6

Printed in the United States of America

Karma, Bhakti, Jnana paths united,
KriyaYoga has integrated.
Action controlled, worship God-centered,
"That I Am?" - be free, surrendered.

Table of Contents

Preface

My purpose in writing this book is to impart the relevence and utility of the multifaceted teachings encapsulated in the relatively small sacred scripture called the Bhagavad Gita to the contemporary householder yogi.

Around 1989, I embarked on the spiritual path of Kriya Yoga, an ancient spiritual practice, re-introduced around 1860 to the spiritual world of Northern India. The renowned representative of Kriya Yoga in the West was Paramhansa Yogananda, the author of the well-known classic *Autobiography of Yoga*.

One of the guidelines laid down by Yogananda's teacher Shri Yukteswar and his teacher, Lahiri Mahasaya, was that a Kriya practitioner should take time each day to read a few passages from the Gita. Of course, you will find that all three of these Yogis have written commentaries on the Gita.

A few years after I began my study of the Gita, I was visiting my favorite bookstore in Berkeley, Serendipity Bookstore, when the owner Peter Howard, asked me whether I was interested in a first printed edition copy of the Indian classic called the Bhagavad Gita. Peter and I had often discussed a wide variety of topics during my past visits which were primarily concerned with Science Fiction and Fantasy First Editions. However, I had also purchased some very old spiritual books from him. From that day onwards, I began my collection of the large numbers of English translations of the Gita. It has been a fascinating journey, perhaps spurred by the thought that I would be able to find the definitive translation or commentary for this highly regarded tome.

The purpose of this text is to explain my understanding of the key concepts and teachings of the Gita in the context of Yoga and especially Kriya Yoga for the householder yogi. It is my hope that it will be helpful to curious as well ardent spiritual seekers. There are many concepts such as karma, dharma, Nishkarma Karma, Bhakti, Jnana, the three Gunas, moksha, dispassion, personal and impersonal God etc. which are sprinkled in different places within the Gita and my goal is to explain the relationships between them that are relevant to someone on the spiritual path. In pursuit of this goal, these concepts are worked through from different perspectives and contexts, and there may seen to be repetition in their usage but with some thought, you will find their relevance from a different angle.

To its admirers, the Bhagavad Gita is one of the world's most important books – a great resource for all of humanity.

Since 1785, when it was translated into English, the Gita has been a powerful influence in the West. The impact has been mostly indirectly through Western philosophers, poets and other literati. The New England Transcendentalists—a loose group of nineteenth-century Americans who were an important school of thinkers and writers that in some respects anticipated later Theosophical thought—read the first English translation of the Gita. Henry David Thoreau, one of that group, wrote about reading the Gita on the shore of Walden Pond, and its philosophy inspired his famous essay, "On Civil Disobedience," about how to cope with societal injustice.

Much later, when Mohandas Gandhi was a young man and a law student in England, he was introduced to the Gita by the Theosophists, after which he read Thoreau's essay, which in turn inspired his policy of *satyagraha* or passive resistance. In turn, Martin Luther King was inspired by Gandhi's policy to create his own program of nonviolence. The Gita has echoed back and forth across the globe between India and America, instigating thought and action on many aspects of contemporary society.

In India, the Gita is now considered the major guidebook to the spiritual life in the "Hindu tradition" or more aptly, Sanatana Dharma. It functioned to unify the diverse views of a plurality of yogic, religious and philosophical traditions. The irony is that this has been actualized only since the publication of the first English translation. Prior to 1785, the Gita, although considered one of the three pillars of Vedanta and as well as a key text of the Krishna Bhakti movement, was not well-known among the common people. It was through the Theosophical influence and then the Indian Nationalist movement that the Gita came to the forefront.

The Bhagavad Gita can be translated as 'The Song of God'. It is a very small part of the greatest and longest epic ever written—the Mahabharata, which recounts the story of a great civil war in Northern India. Epics typically show the values and defining characteristics of a people. The Mahabharata is in that way the quintessential story of India. But it is also the story of all human beings, a universal epic, for it deals with fundamental human motives, frustrations, quandaries, and joys. The Gita is around 700 verses that is from Book 6 (Bhishma Parva) of the Mahabharata.

Spiritually, the Gita is about moksha, or liberation from karma. There is also a religious dimension as well as teachings on moral and ethical conduct. The conceptual framework is a basic theme in the Mahabharata—dharma or the way we should act because of who and what we are. In particular, the Gita is about a moral quandary in which the hero in this civil war faces fundamental questions about the right way to live. The poem operates on two levels—historical and archetypal. It is a history of an actual battle fought near modern Delhi at a turning point in human history. But it is also an archetypal myth about the struggle that each one of us experiences within ourselves. This archetypal nature is amplified by the Kriya Yoga tradition, wherein all the characters in the epic represent human emotional and mental traits.

The dual level of the poem is made clear in the opening two words of the poem: "Dharmakshetre, Kurukshetre," which mean "On the field of dharma, on the Field of the Kurus." The Kurus were the ruling family of India at the time of the poem, and Kurukshetra is an actual geographical location, a field, near modern Delhi where the ancient civil war was fought. So, the second word of the poem tells us that we are dealing with a particular place and time, thousands of years ago, in the heroic age of India.

However, the first word of the poem tells us that we are dealing with a timeless reality. Dharma (a central word in the Gita) means, among other things, the essential nature of a thing or person. And so, the poem is about the "field" or subject matter of what is essentially real in life. It is precisely in this arena that the essays in this book operate.

Introduction

The Structure and Unified Yoga Path of the Bhagavad Gita

The first 6 chapters of the Bhagavad Gita focus on Duty and Action - Karma Yoga path to Self-realization. Chapters 3,4, and 5 are especially relevant for householder yogis enmeshed in day to day life.

The Bhagavad Gita opens with Arjuna in a state of dejection and despair. As he surveys the battlefield, he sees arrayed before him friends, relatives, teachers - people dear to him who he does not wish to fight. Overcome by sorrow and self-doubt, Arjuna tells Krishna that he sees no good in killing his own kinsmen for the sake of a kingdom.

In response, Krishna explains to Arjuna the eternal nature of the soul and the illusion of grief. The soul is immortal and indestructible, taking new bodies through reincarnation. No one can cause the soul to be destroyed. Krishna tells Arjuna that the wise grieve neither for the living nor for the dead, as death is certain for anyone born. We should not sorrow over the inevitable.

Krishna goes on to explain the concept of Karma Yoga. One's duty in life is to carry out sacrificial actions without attachment to the results. Performing action as a service to God frees one from the bondage of Karma. The true renunciation is giving up selfish attachments, not physical action itself. By fixing the mind on the Supreme and performing obligatory actions for His sake, one attains perfection.

In chapter 3, Arjuna asks Krishna which is superior - the path of knowledge or the path of action. Krishna responds that both ultimately lead to the same goal, but the path of action is better suited to Arjuna's nature. The true seeker is one who sees inaction in action, and action in inaction. One must act according to their innate tendencies, without attachment.

Krishna reveals that he taught the science of Karma Yoga in a previous age. It is ancient wisdom passed down through an unbroken tradition. He encourages Arjuna to fight, free from personal desire or aversion. Krishna will free him from sin, as Arjuna's motives are selfless and his intent is pure.

Chapter 4 sees Krishna explain the deeper truths about sacrifice, action, transcendental knowledge and the purpose of creation. Krishna says he is born in every age to re-establish righteousness and relay these spiritual principles. The ignorant, who lack faith, complain when confronted with this knowledge, while the wise accept and attain liberation.

In Chapter 5, Krishna defines the marks of a stable, illumined sage. One who has abandoned selfish attachment, subdued the senses and fixed the mind on the Supreme Self is untouched by external contacts. Freed from egoism and dualities like pleasure and pain, such a yogi acts blissfully for the welfare of all beings. Krishna says this difficult path is attainable through practice and detachment.

Finally, in Chapter 6, Krishna describes the technique of meditative discipline. Sitting upright with body, mind and senses controlled, one must meditate on the Supreme Self within the heart. With practice, the natural disturbances of the mind are reined in. Krishna says if one fails in the path, there is no loss or harm, as no effort towards spiritual growth is ever wasted. Through perseverance, the perfected yogi achieves supreme peace and ultimate union with the Divine.

These first six chapters of the Bhagavad Gita, focused on Karma Yoga as the path to Self-realization and the qualities of the ideal yogi who has achieved equanimity and inner stillness.

Kriya Yoga is considered a form of Karma Yoga as it involves action performed with discipline and detachment as an offering to the Divine. Some examples of how Kriya Yoga embodies the principles of Karma Yoga:

- Kriya Yoga practices like pranayama (breath control), mudras (hand gestures), and dhyana (meditation) involve active effort and discipline of the body and mind. They are performed as sacred action, not for selfish aims.
- The different asanas and postures of Hatha Yoga that comprise Kriya Yoga are a mastery over the body and withdrawal of the senses - key concepts in Karma Yoga.
- Performing Kriya Yoga with an attitude of service and devotion, without attachment to results or egoism, helps release past karma and purify the mind. This aligns with the Karma Yoga philosophy.
- The end goal of Kriya Yoga is inner realization and unity with the Divine, not physical rewards. This non-attachment to fruit of actions makes it Karma Yoga in spirit.
- Kriya Yoga emphasizes skill in action - acting with complete concentration and focus for spiritual evolution. This "yoga of action" is central to Karma Yoga.
- Kriya Yoga practitioners strive to see God in all actions and treat their practice as worship. This transforms mundane deeds into sacred service, or karma as yoga.

In essence, Kriya Yoga incorporates active techniques practiced with discipline, surrender and the right intention or bhava to achieve spiritual growth. By using action as a tool for inner purification, it aligns with the core principles of Karma Yoga.

A summary of chapters 7-12 of the Bhagavad Gita which focus on Bhakti Yoga and attaining God Realization:

In Chapter 7, Lord Krishna reveals that while most seek Him in form, a rare few realize His formless aspect through the path of knowledge. Yet He submits to the devotion of those who worship Him in form: "I am not manifest to all…those who seek Me in forms, to them I carry their desires." (7.21,7.22)

Krishna states He is the origin of all, and everything rests in Him. But His material maya energy veils this from the ignorant. The wise take refuge in Him, striving for liberation from old age and death: "At the end of many lives, the wise resort to Me…" (7.19)

Chapter 8 sees Krishna explain the paths to Brahmaloka, the imperishable highest abode. By remembering God at the time of death, merging into His essence, the yogi is not reborn: "He who…leaves the body while meditating on Me, reaches My state." (8.5)

Krishna describes Brahman, the eternal source of all creation. He is the Lord who pervades and sustains the cosmos. Understanding His indestructible being, the devotees engage in His loving service.

In Chapter 9, Krishna reveals His cosmic form to Arjuna, manifesting time and the infinite universes: "O Arjuna, behold My forms by the hundreds and thousands…" (9.5) Overawed by this vision, Arjuna offers prayers of adoration.

Krishna states that those who worship other gods with faith actually worship Him, though improperly. Sincere devotion ultimately reaches Him: "Whosoever seeks Me, through whatsoever form, I meet them on that path..." (9.23)

Chapter 10 sees Krishna glorify His limitless opulences and supremacy. All wondrous things originate from a fraction of His power. Arjuna is exhorted to adore Him single-mindedly, and Krishna will dispel his fears and worldly sorrows.

In Chapter 11, Arjuna asks to see Krishna's divine form. The Lord reveals His supreme, effulgent, all-encompassing Vishvarupa - the infinite cosmos envisioned in one transcendent form. Arjuna is left awe-struck and offers heartfelt prayers.

Krishna declares that devotion to Him is the sovereign path and highest secret. By wholehearted love, He can be known and realized: "Setting your heart on Me, giving your whole self to Me, you will certainly come to Me." (11.54)

Finally in Chapter 12, Arjuna asks which devotees are most perfect - those who worship the formless Absolute or those who worship the Godhead in form. Krishna answers that those who fix their minds on Him and revere Him with supreme faith excel in yoga. He reassures that He is easily attained through constant devotion.

The essence of chapters 7-12 of the Gita is an emphasis on passionate devotion to the Personal God as the direct path to the Divine.

Chapters 7-12 of the Gita focus on Bhakti Yoga or the path of devotion. This relates to Kriya Yoga in the following ways:

- Kriya Yoga considers devotion and surrender to God as essential. Regular spiritual practice is an expression of Bhakti or loving devotion.
- The aim in both is to realize and connect with the Divine -

Bhakti Yoga emphasizes realizing God with form, Kriya Yoga leads to realization of the formless Absolute.

- Kriya Yoga practices like japa, mantra repetition, and chanting the names of God reflect the Bhakti Yoga elements of worship, prayer and singing glory.
- In Kriya Yoga, the guru is revered as the embodiment of the Divine. Surrender to the guru is a form of Bhakti Yoga's surrender to God.
- Meditation in Kriya Yoga aims at merging the individual soul with the Infinite, similar to Bhakti Yoga's goal of union with the Beloved.
- Kriya Yoga encourages cultivating the 9 forms of Bhakti like listening to discourses, worship seva, spiritual company to deepen devotion.
- Kriya Yoga infuses Bhakti into active Yoga practice. The spirit of devotion transforms mechanical actions into loving service.
- Both paths emphasize loving remembrance of God in daily life and at the time of death for realization.

In essence, Kriya Yoga fuses Karma Yoga's techniques with Bhakti Yoga's devotional fervor to hasten spiritual evolution.

Chapters 13-18 of the Bhagavad Gita which focus on Jnana Yoga, the path of knowledge, and attaining Cosmic Consciousness:

In Chapter 13, Krishna describes the field of activities and the knower of this field. The body is the field, and the soul or consciousness that knows it is the knower. By understanding the difference between material nature and the seer of nature, one attains self-realization.

Krishna explains the path of knowledge - through discernment, one realizes the Supreme Self pervading all things: "When a man sees self-effulgent Self in all beings...that is perception of oneness." (13.30)

Chapter 14 has Krishna discuss the three gunas - sattva, rajas and tamas which comprise all things. With sattva predominant, wisdom arises: "When the seer perceives no agent other than the gunas and knows Him who is higher than the gunas, he attains nirvana." (14.19)

In Chapter 15, Krishna uses the metaphor of an inverted tree to describe creation - the roots are above in the Supreme Self, the branches below are the material world. The Vedas seek to cut this entanglement and lead one to liberation through self-knowledge.

Krishna contrasts the transient material world with His own supreme, imperishable nature. The wise take refuge in Him through love and devotion.

Chapter 16 details the divine and demonic temperaments. But even those established in demonic ways can attain perfection by devotion to the Lord: "Take refuge in Him alone with your whole being, Arjuna...By His grace you will attain supreme peace." (16.62)

In Chapter 17, Krishna elaborates on faith, sacrifice, austerity and charity - acts of worship that purify the mind. He concludes knowledge is sattvic, passion rajasic and ignorance tamasic. With faith in scripture, one's nature is transformed.

Finally in Chapter 18, Krishna reveals that desireless action, renouncing attachment, is true sannyasa. By devotion through one's natural duties, the mind is stilled to prepare for death: "Restraining and subduing the senses...he who acts solely for purification - his karma is sattvic." (18.51)

Krishna urges Arjuna to abandon all dharmas and take complete refuge in Him alone. This will grant supreme bhakti and release from the cycle of rebirth: "Setting your heart on Me, giving your whole self to Me, you will certainly come to Me." (18.65)

This summarizes the Jnana Yoga teachings in chapters 13-18 - the path of transcendental knowledge culminating in the universal God-consciousness.

The Jnana Yoga path of knowledge described in chapters 13-18 relates to Kriya Yoga in the following ways:

- Kriya Yoga aims at both jnana (wisdom) through meditation and vipassana (self-inquiry), as well as bhakti (devotion) through spiritual practices.
- Jnana Yoga's analysis of Nature, gunas, and the difference between matter and spirit aligns with Kriya Yoga's goal of attaining higher states of consciousness.
- Both emphasize stilling the modifications of the mind through self-discipline to attain realization of the true Self.
- Kriya Yoga techniques like Hong-Sau help concentrate the scattered mind in preparation for Self-inquiry. - Jnana Yoga's renunciation of personal desire and identity to unite with the Absolute mirrors the inner renunciation in Kriya Yoga.
- Kriya Yoga stresses the role of the guru in imparting self-knowledge, similar to the guru's guidance in Jnana Yoga.
- Regular meditation in Kriya Yoga cultivates the discernment between the permanent and fleeting, as in Jnana Yoga.
- For the Jnana yogi, action becomes worship. Likewise, Kriya Yoga turns ritual actions into offerings to the Divine.
- Both paths lead to the direct experience of one's eternal iden-

tity with the Supreme Self, merging knower, knowing and known.

So the intellectual inquiry of Jnana Yoga supports the experiential realization generated through Kriya Yoga.

In summary, my contention (refer figure 1) is that the whole of the Gita is a unified yogic path which in modern times is called Kriya Yoga by Lahiri Mahasaya per instruction from the ineffeble Mahavatar Babaji. Kriya Yoga unifies all three parts of the yogic path - Karma, Bhakti and Jnana Yogas.

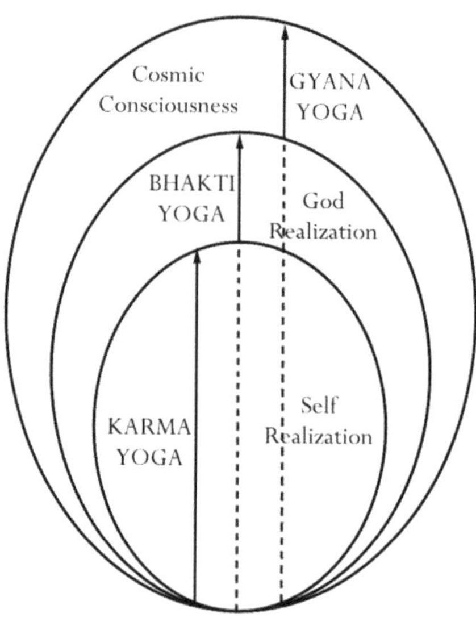

Figure 1: Unified Yogic Path of Gita

The Gita for Householder Yogi

In Kurukshetra, Arjuna filled with sorrow,
Seeing his kinsmen arrayed for war's morrow.

Krishna counseled action without attachment,
This is the practice of Karma Yoga, detachment.
Control thy mind and senses, be steady,
Work is thy duty, results leave to Me ready.

Devotion I praise, take refuge in Me only,
In any form worship, pure, devoted, lonely.
I am Vishnu, cause of creation's motion,
By Bhakti Yoga attain thou divine devotion.

The field and knower I have revealed in stages,
Jnana Yoga illumines, stilling mind's cages.
Three gunas comprise all things moving, inert,
With sattva leading to wisdom, thus assert.

Pranayama, meditation, fire of knowledge,
Kriya Yoga grants experience and cognizance.
Practice its techniques daily without misplacing,
Realize in timelessness, cosmic consciousness embracing.

Control the senses, steady in duty,
Work selflessly, leave results to Me, the Buddhi.
In any form, worship Me devoted,
Bhakti Yoga leads to God realized.

I am Vishnu, the creator, take refuge,
By devotion attain Me without subterfuge.

Pranayama, dhyana, fire of knowledge rare,
Kriya Yoga leads to cosmic awareness fair.
Practice its techniques daily constant,
In timeless realization, mind silent.

Karma, Bhakti, Jnana paths united,
Kriya Yoga has integrated.
Act controlled, worship God-centered,
"That I Am?"- be free, surrendered.

Arjuna saw his kinsmen, was filled with sorrow,
Krishna said: act today, detach from tomorrow.

I'm Vishnu, creator, take refuge Me only,
By devotion attain Me wholly.

Pranayama and meditation of Kriya grand,
Leads one to samadhi, consciousness expanded.
Integrating three paths trod upon,
Kriya Yoga takes seeker beyond.

Act with discipline, worship God lonely,
"Who am I?"- Self-inquiry leads one homely.
Arjuna's plight thereafter Krishna curing,
Wise counsel providing, his sorrow allaying.

Bhagavad Gita and Patanjali's Yoga Sutras

The Bhagavad Gita and Patanjali's Yoga Sutras are two of the most influential scriptures that have shaped the practices and philosophies of yoga. Though different in structure and content, they share some core teachings and values.

The Gita is a sacred text of the Sanatana Dharma that is part of the epic Mahabharata. It takes the form of a dialogue between the warrior Arjuna and his charioteer Krishna on the battlefield before a great war. Krishna counsels Arjuna on his duties as a warrior and expounds on a number of yogic and Vedantic philosophies. Central to the Gita is the idea of dharmic action - acting according to one's sacred duties without attachment to the outcome. As Krishna says:

"You have a right to perform your prescribed duties, but you are not entitled to the fruits of your actions. Never consider yourself to be the cause of the results of your activities, nor be attached to inaction." (Gita, 2.47)

The Yoga Sutras of Patanjali are a collection of 196 aphorisms or threads on the theory and practice of yoga. Patanjali outlines an eight-limbed (ashtanga) system of yoga, moving from moral disciplines to postures to meditation and absorption. A core teaching is that of stilling the fluctuations of the mind through concentration and detachment. As Patanjali states:

Yoga is the inhibition of the modifications of the mind. (Yoga Sutras, 1.2), and -

When the mind maintains awareness, yet does not mingle with the senses, nor the senses with sense impressions, then self-awareness blossoms. (Yoga Sutras, 2.54)

While the Gita covers a wide range of spiritual topics and philosophies, the Patanjali's focus is on the theory and practice of yoga, with a more clinical and structured approach. The Gita has dialogues, stories, metaphors, and descriptions, while the Sutras are terse and precise statements.

However, there are several core themes and teachings found in both:

- The path to liberation: Both scriptures view the purpose of yoga and spiritual practice as liberation (moksha) from worldly suffering and the cycle of rebirth. The Gita focuses on attaining liberation through selfless action (the result of yoga meditation), devotion to God/Krishna and light of wisdom, while Patanjali emphasizes liberation through detachment, stilling the fluctuations of the mind, and samadhi or absorption.

- Discipline of the mind and senses: Both emphasize disciplining and controlling the mind and senses in order to realize the true Self. Krishna counsels Arjuna to "deliver yourself with the self" by strengthening his resolve and self-discipline (Gita 6.5). Similarly, Patanjali outlines practices to withdraw the senses and calm mental disturbances.

- Karma yoga and nishkam karma: The Gita introduces the

idea of karma yoga - dedication of one's actions to God without seeking rewards. This relates to Patanjali's teachings on non-attachment (vairagya) - performing actions without egoistic motives.

- The guidance of a guru: Both scriptures emphasize the importance of a guru or teacher who can guide the student in their spiritual practice. Krishna assumes the role of Arjuna's guru, while Patanjali advises taking help and instructions from an advanced yogi or directly from Ishwar (the Divine Guide).
- Paths to transcendence: The Gita outlines jnana (wisdom), bhakti (devotion) and karma (selfless action) as tripartite yogic paths to achieve Cosmic Consciousness. Patanjali does not focus on bhakti but gives surrender to the Godhead (Ishvar Pranidhana) as a requirement to the transcendence through samadhi - absorption of the mind into higher states beyond thought and sensations.

Overall, while the two texts differ significantly in structure, style and emphasis, they share fundamental concepts of Sanatana Dharma and yogic teachings that the path to spiritual awakening requires discipline, renunciation of ego and absorption in something larger than oneself - whether through devotion, selfless action or meditative focus.

Together, they provide philosophical grounding and practical guidance for spiritual aspirants on the yogic path. The appear divergent in methods, but actually are very similar and offer two invaluable resources for liberation of the soul.

The Gita and Yoga Sutras on Sankhya Philosophy

The Bhagavad Gita and Patanjali's Yoga Sutras incorporate and differ from Sankhya philosophy:

Sankhya is one of the six orthodox schools of Hindu philosophy. It was founded by the sage Kapila and is considered one of the oldest philosophical systems in India. The central tenant of Sankhya philosophy is dualism - the existence of two distinct realities, Purusha and Prakriti.

Purusha refers to pure consciousness or the eternal spirit. Prakriti refers to primordial matter or nature, comprised of three qualities (gunas) - goodness (sattva), passion (rajas), and ignorance (tamas). According to Sankhya, it is the interplay between Purusha and Prakriti that leads to the manifestation of the universe and material reality. Liberation occurs when Purusha realizes its distinction from Prakriti and its eternal nature.

The Bhagavad Gita incorporates and builds upon these Sankhya concepts:

- Dualism - The Gita posits two entities that are eternal - the indivisible soul (Atman) and the Divine (Bhagavan). This aligns with Sankhya's two separate realities of Purusha and Prakriti. As Krishna states: There are two entities in this world, the destructible and the indestructible. All creatures are destructible, the unchanging is called indestructible. (Gita 15.16)

- Gunas - The three gunas feature prominently in the Gita as binding the soul to matter. Krishna explains how dominance of each guna leads to different tendencies: Goodness, passion, ignorance - these three qualities, sattva, rajas, tamas, bind the imperishable soul to the perishable body. (Bhagavad Gita 14.5)

However, the Gita differs significantly from classical Sankhya in depicting Purusha and Prakriti as dependent on a higher Divine Reality, Bhagavan or Brahman. Sankhya believes Purusha and Prakriti to be independent realities, but the Gita portrays them as manifestations of the supreme Brahman.

Patanjali's Yoga Sutras have a closer adherence to Sankhya philosophy, though with some variations:

- Dualism - The Sutras posit a distinction between Purusha (pure consciousness) and Prakriti (primordial matter), stating "The primal cause is Brahman. It is undifferentiated, eternal, pure awareness." (YS 1.24). However, in contrast to classical Sankhya, Patanjali equates Purusha with Brahman.
- Gunas - The three gunas feature prominently as obstacles to samadhi. "The fluctuations of consciousness are subdued through meditation on the Triple Gunas devoid of attributes." (YS 2.19)
- Kaivalya - The end goal of yoga in the Sutras is kaivalya, the realization of the distinction between consciousness (Purusha) and materiality (Prakriti). This aligns with Sankhya's concept of liberation. "In the infinite knowledge of Brahman, when the seer sees no longer, that is kaivalya - absolute freedom." (YS 2.25)

However, Patanjali's system also diverges from Sankhya in significant ways:

- Ishvara - Sankhya is silent on the idea of God, whereas Patanjali introduces the concept of Ishvara as a special Purusha that is eternally free. He states that devotion to Ishvara is one path to samadhi.
- Psychology - The Sutras give greater emphasis to the psychic centers (chakras) and occult powers that can arise from meditation. This psychological component is largely absent in Sankhya.
- Ethics - Sankhya focuses on metaphysical knowledge for liberation. But Patanjali emphasizes ethical virtues and moral conduct as part of the eight-limbed path of yoga.

To summarize, the Bhagavad Gita and Yoga Sutras incorporated core Sankhya concepts like dualism, gunas, and bondage of the soul, while modifying them to reconcile with Vedantic philosophy. The Gita emphasizes devotion to a personal God, while Patanjali's psychology, God concept, and ethics exceeded classical Sankhya. While relying on its metaphysical grounding, they tailored Sankhya to the practice-oriented paths of karma yoga and ashtanga yoga. The shared foundation shows Sankhya's seminal influence, while the variations highlight the Gita and Sutra's syntheses of diverse philosophies into integral systems.

The Teachings From The Gita Relevant To The Modern Householder Yogi

Dance of Free Will and Karma

In the Gita, Lord Krishna imparts profound wisdom to Arjuna on various topics - including the nature of reality, the self, and the path to liberation. One of the central teachings in the Gita is the concept of free will and the importance of individual choice in shaping one's actions and destiny. Krishna emphasizes that while he has provided guidance and knowledge, it is ultimately up to Arjuna to make his own decisions and take responsibility for his actions.

The Gita explores the idea of free will through several verses and examples. Here are a few key points:

1. The importance of discernment and decision-making:

In Chapter 2, Verse 47, Krishna tells Arjuna, "You have the right to perform your prescribed duty only, but never to lay claim to its results. Do not become instrumental in making your actions bear fruit, nor let your attachment be to inaction."

This verse highlights the significance of performing one's duty without attachment to the outcome. It emphasizes the need for individuals to exercise their judgment and make choices based on their understanding of righteousness.

2. The power to choose action or inaction:

In Chapter 3, Verse 5, Krishna states, "Nobody can stay without performing actions even for a moment - indeed, all beings are compelled to act by their innate tendencies."

This verse emphasizes that action is an inherent aspect of human existence, and inaction is not a viable option. However, Krishna does not force Arjuna to act in any specific way. Instead, he empowers Arjuna to exercise his free will and choose the course of action that aligns with his understanding and duty.

3. The need to surrender to the divine will:

While the Gita teaches the importance of free will, it also emphasizes the surrender of one's actions and their fruits to a higher power. In Chapter 18, Verse 66, Krishna advises Arjuna, "Abandon all varieties of dharma and simply surrender to Me. I shall liberate you from all sinful reactions. Don't fear." This verse suggests that true liberation comes through surrendering to the divine will and trusting in the guidance of a higher power, while still making individual choices in line with one's duty.

Krishna's message in the Gita is a harmonious integration of free will and surrender. He encourages individuals to exercise their discernment and make choices based on their understanding of righteousness and duty, while also acknowledging the importance of surrendering to the higher divine will. The Gita teaches that one can act freely while remaining aware of the interconnectedness of all beings and the divine order governing the universe.

In the context of the Bhagavad Gita, free will and karma are interconnected concepts. Karma refers to the law of cause and effect, where every action has consequences that determine one's future experiences and circumstances. The Gita recognizes that individuals have the freedom to make choices, but those choices are not entirely independent of their past actions and the consequences that arise from them.

Arjuna, as a warrior, has a karmic duty to fulfill. However, when he is faced with the prospect of fighting in the Kurukshetra war, he becomes overwhelmed by compassion and moral dilemmas, leading him to question the righteousness of engaging in battle. In this situation, Arjuna's free will comes into play. He has the choice to either fulfill his karmic duty as a warrior or to abstain from the fight.

Krishna guides Arjuna by providing him with profound wisdom to help him make an informed decision. The Gita teaches that while individuals have the freedom to choose their actions, they cannot escape the consequences of their past actions, which is governed by their karma. Krishna advises Arjuna to focus on performing his duty without attachment to the results.

This teaching implies that Arjuna is accountable for his actions and their consequences, including the karmic implications. If Arjuna chooses to fulfill his duty as a warrior and fights in the war with a sense of duty and righteousness, he will incur the karmic consequences of his actions, whether positive or negative. Similarly, if he chooses to abstain from the battle, he will also bear the consequences of that choice.

The Gita encourages individuals to act in alignment with their Swadharma, their inherent duty and nature, while being aware of the karmic implications. The emphasis is on performing actions selflessly, without attachment to the fruits of those actions, and surrendering the results to a higher power.

Ultimately, the Gita suggests that while individuals have free will to make choices, they should do so in accordance with their duty and with an understanding of the karmic repercussions. By acting selflessly and surrendering to the divine will, one can navigate the complexities of free will and karma, seeking to fulfill their responsibilities while maintaining spiritual growth and liberation. (Refer to figure 2 below)

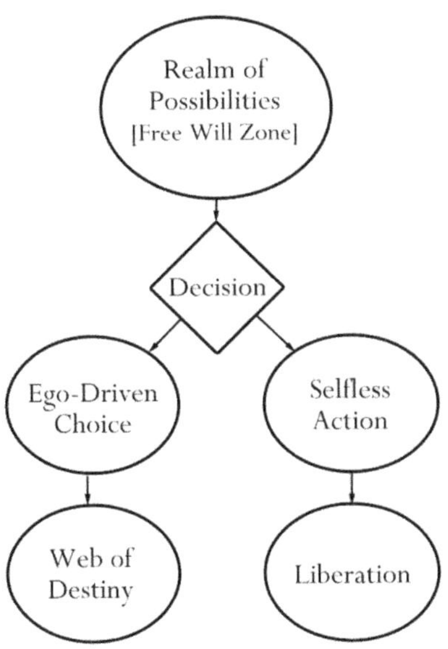

Figure 2: Free Will and Karma

Free Will

In subtle realm where fate and deeds entwine,
Where mortals ponder paths, their lives define,
The dance of free will and karma is a fight,
In realms unseen, veiled by eternal light.

A hero stands, with choices to be made,
His soul, a tapestry, by choices swayed.
To fight or flee, to heed the warrior's call,
His duty bound, amidst life's rise and fall.

Yet destiny's thread, in karma's subtle flow,
Weaves consequences that the wise shall know.
Each action, ripple in the cosmic sea,
A tapestry of deeds, a symphony.

For choices made, with freedom's sacred reign,
Bear fruits, borne from past and present claim.
In lives long past, the echoes still resound,
As karmic chains, in each step, are found.

Oh, free will's gift, a blessing and a test,
A path where souls encounter what is best.
To seek the righteous way, with open heart,
And face the consequences – such an art.

In Swadharma's embrace, the soul may find,
The balance of free will and fate aligned.
To act with love, with righteousness as guide,
And trust the cosmic order, deep and wide

So let us walk this path, with spirits bright,
Embracing free will's flame, a beacon light.
For in the realm where choices ebb and flow,
Karma's tapestry unfolds, and we shall grow.

Overcoming Karma by Selfless Dharma

Karma, its significance and mitigation in the spiritual practitioner's life is a constant thread running through the Gita.

Here are some key teachings on karma from the Gita, along with appropriate verses as examples:

1. Law of Cause and Effect:

   Whatever action a great man performs, common men follow. And whatever standards he sets by exemplary acts, all the world pursues. (Gita 3.21)

This verse highlights that our actions influence others and set an example. It emphasizes the importance of performing righteous deeds as they create a positive impact on society.

2. Duty and Selfless Action:

   "You have the right to perform your prescribed duty, but you are not entitled to the fruits of your actions. (Gita 2.47)

Here, Lord Krishna advises Arjuna that one should focus on fulfilling their responsibilities or duties without being attached to the outcomes. The emphasis is on performing actions selflessly, without expecting personal gains.

3. Law of Reciprocity:

   > People worship me for different reasons and I fulfill their desires accordingly. They approach me with different motives. (Gita 4.11)

This verse highlights the principle of karma, which states that our actions have consequences. Our present actions shape our future experiences, and we bear the fruits of our deeds accordingly.

4. The three mental afflictions that lead to negative actions which in turn result in negative karma:

   > There are three gates leading to the hell of self-destruction for the soul: lust, anger, and greed. Therefore, one must learn to give up these three.(Gita 16.21)

This verse points out the detrimental actions driven by negative emotions. It emphasizes the need to avoid actions motivated by lust, anger, and greed, as they lead to negative consequences.

5. Detachment and Renunciation:

   > A person can rise through the efforts of his own mind; he can also degrade himself, by his own mind. Because mind is the friend of the conditioned soul, and his enemy as well. (Gita 6.5)

Here, Lord Krishna emphasizes the importance of controlling the mind and developing detachment. By disciplining the mind and detaching oneself from the fruits of actions, one can rise above the cycle of karma.

These teachings provide insights to navigate through the karmic minefield and offer guidance on leading a righteous and purposeful life.

Lord Krishna also imparts teachings on dharma, which refers to one's duty or righteous path in life. Here are some key teachings on dharma from the Gita, along with appropriate verses:

1. Fulfilling One's Duty and finding out one's dharma in life:

   It is better to perform one's own duties imperfectly than to master the duties of someone else. By fulfilling the obligations born of their nature, one does not incur sin. (Gita 18.47)

Here, Lord Krishna emphasizes the importance of fulfilling one's own duties according to one's inherent nature and abilities. It suggests that it is better to perform one's own duty to the best of one's ability rather than trying to perform someone else's duty. Therefore, it is important to recognize and follow one's own dharma or duty, even if we may initially seem ill-suited. It emphasizes the significance of understanding one's inherent nature and acting accordingly.

2. Duty Without Attachment:

   You have the right to perform your prescribed duty, but you are not entitled to the fruits of your actions. Never consider yourself the cause of the results of your activities, and never be attached to not doing your duty. (Gita 2.47)

This verse highlights the idea of performing one's duty without attachment to the outcomes. It emphasizes the need to focus on the action itself, rather than being attached to the rewards or results.

3. Upholding Righteousness:

   When righteousness is weak and faints, and unrighteousness exults in pride, then my Spirit arises on Earth. (Gita 4.7)

Lord Krishna reassures humanity that whenever righteousness declines and unrighteousness prevail, the divine spirit manifests itself to restore righteousness and bring balance to the world.

4. Surrendering to the Divine Will is ultimate dharma:

   Abandon all varieties of religion and just surrender unto Me. I shall deliver you from all sinful reactions. Do not fear. (Gita 18.66)

The spiritual practitioner is encouraged to cultivate surrendering to the divine will and placing trust in the Supreme. It suggests that by surrendering to the ultimate reality, one can be liberated from the cycle of birth and death. This can be considered the ultimate dharma for all of humanity.

These teachings on dharma from the Bhagavad Gita offer guidance on leading a righteous and purposeful life by understanding one's duty, performing it selflessly, upholding righteousness, and surrendering to the divine will.

Karma and dharma are closely interconnected concepts that are intricately linked. Here are some ways in which karma and dharma are related:

1. Duty and Karma:

   Karma refers to actions and their consequences, while dharma signifies one's righteous duty or path in life. The Gita emphasizes the importance of performing one's duty (dharma) without attachment to the outcomes (karma).

   You have the right to perform your prescribed duty, but you are not entitled to the fruits of your actions. Never consider yourself the cause of the results of your activities, and never be attached to not doing your duty. (Gita 2.47)

2. Dharma and Righteous Action:

   Dharma guides individuals in choosing the right actions that align with their responsibilities and inherent nature. Performing actions in accordance with dharma leads to positive karma and spiritual growth.

   When one's intelligence, mind, faith and refuge are all fixed in the Supreme, then one becomes fully cleansed of misgivings through complete knowledge and thus proceeds straight on the path of liberation. (Gita 5.17)

3. Law of Cause and Effect:

   The concept of karma in the Gita reinforces the principle that every action, whether in accordance with dharma or not, has consequences. Actions performed against dharma result in negative karma, while actions in alignment with dharma lead to positive karma.

Gita 4.11 as per law of reciprocity

4. Dharma and Liberation:

   Following one's dharma and performing righteous actions ultimately leads to spiritual growth, self-realization, and liberation from the cycle of birth and death. By fulfilling one's duties selflessly, one can purify their karma and progress on the path of enlightenment.

   Better is one's own duty, though imperfectly performed, than the duty of another well-performed. Performing the duty prescribed by one's own nature, one incurs no sin. (Gita 18.47)

In summary, karma and dharma are interconnected in the Gita, with dharma guiding individuals to perform righteous actions in alignment with their responsibilities and inherent nature. By fulfilling their duties selflessly, individuals can purify their karma, progress spiritually, and ultimately attain liberation.

Karma and Dharma

In sacred verses, Gita's wisdom unfolds,
A tapestry of truths, timeless and bold.
In rhythmic dance of words, we find our way,
To grasp the teachings that the Lord conveys.

Karma, the law that binds our actions tight,
As deeds beget results, both dark and bright.
Each choice we make, a ripple in life's stream,
A web of consequences, what a dream.

"Perform thy duty, without fruits desired,"
The Gita speaks, as guidance is inspired.
Detach thyself from outcomes and rewards,
True essence lies in actions, not in hoards.

Dharma, the path that leads to righteous grace,
In duties fulfilled, we find our rightful place.
Discover your own nature, duty's call,
For in this sacred quest, we stand tall.

"Abandon not your duty, fear not the weight,"
The Gita sounds, words to contemplate.
Uphold the righteous path with strength and might,
Through dharma's lens, the world is bathed in light.

Karma and dharma, intertwined they dance,
In harmony, life's purpose they enhance.
Through actions just and duties well embraced,
The soul transcends, in divine love encased.

So let us heed the Lord for ever more,
And tread the path of righteousness once more.
With karma's weight and dharma as our guide,
In harmony with life, our light we reside

Description of the Ideal Yogi

Some of the most instructive passages in the Gita concern the attributes of an Ideal Yogi. The Gita describes the practice of yoga as a path to self-realization and union with the divine. Therefore the attributes of an ideal yogi are congruent with that goal:

1. Equanimity: An ideal yogi remains calm and composed in all situations. They are not affected by the dualities of life, such as pleasure and pain, success and failure, and praise and criticism. They maintain a balanced and steady mind.

   "Perform your duty with equipose, O Arjuna, abandoning all attachment to success or failure. Such equanimity is called yoga." 2:48

2. Self-discipline: A yogi practices self-discipline and self-control. They regulate their thoughts, actions, and senses, cultivating restraint and moderation in all aspects of life.

   "A person is said to be established in self-realization and is called a yogi when he is fully satisfied by virtue of acquired knowledge and realization. Such a person is situated in transcendence and is self-controlled. He sees everything—whether it be pebbles, stones or gold—as the same." 5:8

3. Renunciation: The Gita emphasizes the importance of renunciation, which does not necessarily mean giving up worldly possessions, but rather cultivating a detachment

from the fruits of one's actions. An ideal yogi performs their duties without attachment to the outcomes.

"Before giving up this present body, if one is able to tolerate the urges of the material senses and check the force of desire and anger, he is well situated and is happy in this world." 6:23

4. Selflessness: The Gita emphasizes the value of selflessness and service. An ideal yogi works for the welfare of others without seeking personal gain or recognition. They act with compassion and kindness towards all beings.

   "He who is not envious but is a kind friend to all living entities, who does not think himself a proprietor, who is free from false ego and equal both in happiness and distress, who is always satisfied and engaged in devotional service with determination and whose mind and intelligence are in agreement with Me—he is very dear to Me." 12:13

5. Devotion: The Gita describes different paths of yoga, and one of them is the path of devotion or Bhakti Yoga. An ideal yogi has unwavering devotion and love for the divine. They engage in spiritual practices and rituals as an expression of their love and surrender.

   "To those who are constantly devoted and who engage in the devotional service with faith, love, and concentration, I give the understanding by which they can come to Me." 9:22

6. Wisdom and Knowledge: An ideal yogi seeks wisdom

and self-knowledge. They cultivate a deep understanding of the true nature of the self and the universe. They constantly strive to expand their knowledge through study, contemplation, and reflection.

7. Fearlessness: A yogi is fearless and unshaken by the challenges and obstacles of life. They have faith in the divine order and trust that everything happens for a reason. They face difficulties with courage and resilience.

   "He who is temperate in his habits of eating, sleeping, working, and recreation can mitigate all material pains by practicing the yoga system." 6:17

8. Meditation and Contemplation: The Gita highlights the importance of meditation and contemplation for self-realization. An ideal yogi regularly practices meditation to still the mind, attain inner peace, and connect with the divine consciousness.

It's important to note that the Gita presents these attributes as ideals to aspire to, recognizing that the path of yoga is a journey of self-discovery and spiritual growth. Different individuals may exhibit these attributes to varying degrees, and the emphasis on each attribute may vary depending on the individual's nature and chosen path of yoga. It is also important to read these verses in the context of the entire scripture to gain a comprehensive understanding of the teachings.

The Yogi

By ancient ways, a soul emerged, serene and wise,
In tranquil depths of yogic grace, it reached the skies.
With tranquil mind and steadfast heart, it sought the truth,
Embracing virtue's noble path, a living proof.

In equipoise, it faced the world, undisturbed by strife,
Detached from fruits of actions, living a humble life.
Self-discipline adorned its days, with passions tamed,
Restraining senses, mastering self, it overcame.

Through acts of selflessness, it served with love and care,
Compassion flowing freely, a balm to all despair.
Devotion burned like sacred fire, an eternal flame,
Bathing in divine love, it called the sacred name.

In wisdom's realm, it roamed, seeking the inner light,
Diving deep into the soul's depths, a mystic sight.
The secrets of existence unveiled with each breath,
Revealing unity's embrace, life's cosmic breadth.

Fearless it stood, amidst the storms life did unfold,
Trusting the divine order, with destinies are foretold.
With steadfast mind, it meditated, a sacred art,
In stillness, finding solace, unity of heart.

Thus, the ideal yogi lived, a beacon of grace,
Treading the path of liberation, conquering the maze.
With every step, it soared to realms beyond the skies,
Transcending mortal limitations, to where spirit flies.

In this sacred tale, we find a guiding light,
The yogi's attributes, shining with radiant might.
Let us embrace these noble traits, in life's grand quest,
And strive to be the yogi true, in heart and rest.

In cyclic realms of yore, a yogi's spirit soared,
A symphony of virtues, a divine accord.
With breath of peace, it walked upon this earthly stage,
A living embodiment of wisdom, age by age.

Eyes that beheld a universe, it saw beyond,
Discerning truth in shadows, where illusions spawned.
Through veils of maya, it pierced, to realms unseen,
Revealing unity's tapestry, a sacred dream.

With boundless love, it served the world with open heart,
Each action, selfless offering, a noble art.
In giving, it received, in kindness, found its wealth,
An oasis of compassion, nurturing life's health.

In stillness, it communed with realms of cosmic grace,
Meditative currents guiding to a sacred space.
In silence, it heard whispers of the eternal song,
Union with the divine, where souls belong.

Detached from fleeting fruits, it danced through joy and strife,
With equanimity, embracing every life.
Constant as the sun, never for to stray,
It stood as steadfast witness, undeterred by fray.

In knowledge's embrace, it quenched its thirsting soul,
Seeking the inner truths that make existence whole.
With wisdom's torch ablaze, it cast away the dark,
Awakening the dormant flame, a divine spark.

The ideal yogi, radiant in every way,
A lighthouse in the tempest, guiding night to day.
A beacon of serenity, amidst life's swell,
An embodiment of love, in which we all can dwell.

So let us strive to embody these sacred hues,
To walk the yogi's path, with hearts and minds infused.
For in the ideal yogi's grace, we find our own,
A journey of self-realization, karmic seeds sown.

The Power of Sacrifice

Sacrifice (yajna) is another major theme in the Gita. Looking at sacrifice from a traditional perspective, there are three main types of yajna that are mentioned. These are:

1. Devara yajna: This refers to the worship of the gods or the deities. It involves offering of oblations or offerings to the gods in the form of mantras, prayers, and hymns. This type of yajna is a form of devotion to the divine and is aimed at seeking blessings from the gods.

2. Pitru yajna: This refers to the worship of the ancestors or forefathers. It involves offering of oblations to the ancestors in the form of food and water. This type of yajna is a way of expressing gratitude towards one's ancestors and seeking their blessings.

3. Manushya yajna: This refers to the sacrifice or service to fellow human beings. It involves performing acts of kindness and charity towards others, such as helping the needy, giving food to the hungry, and offering shelter to the homeless. This type of yajna is considered to be a way of promoting social harmony and balance, and is aimed at achieving spiritual growth through selfless service.

In addition to these three main types of yajna, the Bhagavad Gita also mentions other forms of sacrifice, such as the sacrifice of wealth, false knowledge (ignorance) , and one's own ego:

a. Sacrifice of Material Possessions:

In Chapter 17, Verse 20, Lord Krishna describes the sacrifice of material possessions:

"Charity given out of duty, without expectation of return, at the proper time and place, and to a worthy person, is considered to be in the mode of goodness."

According to this verse, sacrificing material possessions through acts of charity is considered a noble form of sacrifice. It emphasizes selflessness, detachment from material wealth, and a sense of duty towards helping others.

b. Sacrifice of Ego:

In Chapter 18, Verse 42, Lord Krishna speaks of the sacrifice of ego:

"And that sacrifice which is performed by men aspiring for liberation, who do not desire the fruits of their actions and who have renounced all attachment, is said to be in the mode of goodness."

This verse highlights the importance of sacrificing one's ego and personal desires for the sake of spiritual growth. It involves letting go of the attachment to the outcomes of one's actions and cultivating a sense of detachment.

c. Sacrifice of ignorance through the fire of Knowledge:

In Chapter 4, Verse 33, Lord Krishna speaks about the sacrifice of knowledge:

"Just as the blazing fire turns firewood to ashes, O Arjuna,

> so does the fire of knowledge burn to ashes all reactions to material activities."
>
> This verse suggests that sacrificing ignorance through the acquisition and application of knowledge is a transformative sacrifice. It refers to the process of gaining spiritual wisdom and understanding, which leads to the destruction of the karmic reactions of one's actions.

The goal of all forms of yajna is to purify one's mind, achieve spiritual growth, and attain union with the divine. In fact, the Gita presents yoga as a form of yajna, and emphasizes the importance of performing all actions as a form of sacrifice to the divine:

Firstly, the Gita teaches that the practice of yoga involves offering oneself to the divine. In other words, yoga is seen as a form of self-surrender or self-offering to the ultimate reality, which is identified as the Supreme Lord or Krishna. This is in line with the concept of yajna, which involves offering of oneself and one's actions to the divine.

Secondly, the Gita teaches that all actions, including the practice of yoga, should be performed as a form of sacrifice to the divine. This means that one should perform all actions with a sense of detachment and offer the fruits of those actions to the divine rather than seeking personal gain or reward. This is also in line with the concept of yajna, which involves performing actions without attachment to the results, and offering the results of those actions to the divine.

Thirdly, the Gita teaches that the ultimate goal of yoga is to attain union with the divine, which is identified as the ultimate sacrifice. In other words, the practice of yoga is seen as a means of achieving spiritual growth and enlightenment, which involves the sacrifice of one's ego and personal desires. This is in line with the spiritual concept of yajna, which involves the sacrifice of one's personal desires and ego in order to attain union with the divine.

Here are some quotes from the Bhagavad Gita that illustrate the connection between yoga and sacrifice:

1. "The meaning of sacrifice is giving up the desire for personal reward. All actions performed with this attitude of sacrifice become yoga." - Bhagavad Gita 4.23

2. "The one who sees inaction in action, and action in inaction, is a wise person. Such a person is a yogi and has accomplished everything through the performance of all actions as a sacrifice to the divine." - Bhagavad Gita 4.18

3. "O Arjuna, offer all your actions to me with a pure heart, free from desire for the fruits of those actions. This is the yoga of selfless action, and it leads to liberation." - Bhagavad Gita 9.27

4. "Those who are established in self-realization and perform all their actions as a sacrifice to the divine, are untouched by the results of those actions. Such people attain supreme peace and happiness." - Bhagavad Gita 5.12

5. "One who is fully absorbed in the practice of yoga sees the self in all beings and all beings in the self. Such a person sees the same divine presence in everything, and thus performs all actions as a sacrifice to that divine presence." - Bhagavad Gita 6.29

Although, it may seem repetitive, it is instructive to once again emphasize that these quotes show that the practice of yoga involves offering oneself and one's actions as a sacrifice to the divine, and that this attitude of selfless action is essential for achieving spiritual growth and liberation:

a. Spiritual Growth and Liberation:

In Chapter 4, Verse 33, Lord Krishna states:

"When you understand the truth of sacrifice, your heart will be cleansed of impurities, and you will attain liberation."

This verse suggests that through sincere and selfless sacrifice, one purifies their heart and attains spiritual growth. It leads to liberation from the cycle of birth and death, enabling one to merge with the Divine.

b. Attainment of Divine Grace:

In Chapter 9, Verse 22, Lord Krishna explains:

"To those who are constantly devoted and who engage in the right ways of sacrifice, I give the understanding by which they can come to Me."

Here, Lord Krishna emphasizes that sincere and dedicated sacrifice leads to divine grace and spiritual enlightenment. It implies that by offering our actions and intentions to the Divine, we receive blessings and guidance on the path of self-realization.

The Gita outlines the process of sacrifice through the concepts of karma yoga and bhakti yoga:

a. **Karma Yoga – Sacrifice through Selfless Action:**

Karma yoga, the yoga of selfless action, is described in Chapter 3, Verse 9:

"You should perform your prescribed duty, for doing so is better than not working. By working sincerely, one can attain the Supreme."

The Gita teaches that sacrifice can be practiced by performing one's duties without attachment to the results. By dedicating actions to the Divine, offering the fruits of labor, and working selflessly for the welfare of others, individuals can engage in the path of sacrifice

Therefore, although yoga is not specifically portrayed as a sacrifice itself, but rather as a means to attain self-realization and ultimately liberation, the practice of yoga, especially karma yoga and bhakti yoga, needs to incorporate the concept of sacrifice.

b. Bhakti Yoga - Sacrifice through Devotion:

Bhakti yoga is the path of devotion and love for the Divine. It involves cultivating a deep connection with God through prayer, worship, and surrender. In the practice of bhakti yoga, individuals offer their thoughts, emotions, and actions to the Divine, considering them as acts of sacrifice.

> In Chapter 9, Verse 26, Lord Krishna explains the essence of bhakti yoga:
>
> "If one offers Me with love and devotion a leaf, a flower, a fruit, or water, I will accept it."
>
> This verse highlights that even simple offerings made with pure love and devotion are considered as sacrifices to the Divine. Bhakti yoga encourages individuals to surrender their ego and desires, offering everything they have in service and devotion to God.

Both of the above paths emphasize selflessness, detachment from personal desires, and the offering of one's actions, intentions, and devotion to a higher power. By engaging in these yogic practices, individuals can cultivate a spirit of sacrifice, leading to spiritual growth, liberation, and union with the Divine.

Liberation through Sacrifice

In sacred Gita's verse, sacrifice blooms bright,
A selfless act, a beacon in the night.
It calls for giving without thought of gain,
Detaching from desires that cause us pain.

Three forms it takes, these offerings we share,
Material possessions, love, and care.
To aid the needy, with open hearts, we give,
Let not selfishness and greed, us to deceive.

As flames devour the wood, so knowledge burns,
Igniting souls, karmic lessons it turns.
To sacrifice ignorance, seek wisdom's light,
For truth's fire shall set our spirits alight.

Through karma's path, with actions selfless, pure,
Our duty done, fruits offered, we endure.
In serving others, higher purpose found,
The ego slain, liberation unbound.

With bhakti's love, devotion's sweet embrace,
A sacrifice of self, a state of grace.
With heartfelt offerings, however small,
We find communion, surrendering all.

In the Lord's wisdom song, sacrifice shines,
A tapestry of love that intertwines.
It purifies the soul, sets spirits free,
Guiding us toward divine unity.

Challenge to Overcome Maya

There is quite a lot that we can learn about the nature of Maya from the Gita. Here are twelve verses that help us in understanding to overcome the worldly illusion and connect with reality:

1. Chapter 7, Verse 14

   Deluded by the three modes [goodness, passion, and ignorance], the whole world does not know Me - who am above them and inexhaustible.

2. Chapter 7, Verse 25:

   I am never manifest to the foolish and unintelligent. For them, I am covered by My eternal creative potency [Maya], and so the deluded world knows Me not, who am unborn and infallible.

3. Chapter 9, Verse 7:

   O son of Kunti, at the end of a cycle, all material manifestation enters into My nature, and at the beginning of another cycle, by Maya, I again create.

4. Chapter 9, Verse 8:

   The whole cosmic order is under Me. By My will it is manifested again and again, and by My will it is annihilated at the end.

5. Chapter 9, Verse 19:

I am the father of this universe, the mother, the support, and the grandsire. I am the object of knowledge, the purifier, and the syllable Om. I am also the Rik, the Sama, and the Yajur [Vedas].

6. Chapter 14, Verse 2:

   Those who have relied on this knowledge attain unity with Me and will not be born at creation or be afflicted at dissolution.

7. Chapter 14, Verse 5:

   The three Gunas or states of material world - goodness, activity and inactivity, bind the eternal embodied one to the body, O Arjuna.

8. Chapter 14, Verse 26:

   One who engages in full devotional service, who does not fall down in any circumstance, at once transcends the modes of material nature and thus comes to the level of Brahman.

9. Chapter 15, Verse 6:

   That supreme abode of Mine is not illumined by the sun or moon, nor by fire or electricity. Those who reach it never return to this material world.

10. Chapter 15, Verse 7:

    The living entities in this conditioned world are My eternal, fragmental parts. Due to conditioned life, they are struggling very hard with the five senses and the mind.

11. Chapter 15, Verse 8:

    The living entity in the material world carries his different conceptions of life from one body to another as the air carries aromas.

12. 1 Chapter 15, Verse 15:

    I am seated in everyone's heart, and from Me come remembrance, knowledge, and forgetfulness. By all the Vedas, I am to be known. Indeed, I am the compiler of Vedanta, and I am the knower of the Vedas."

These verses provide insights into the nature of Maya, the illusionary energy that covers our understanding of the Supreme and binds us to the material world. They also highlight the transcendental position of the Supreme Being and the process of attaining liberation from the influence of Maya through devotional service.

Let's study in more detail, the Lord's teachings about Maya, its origin, effects, and methods to overcome it:

1. Nature of Maya: Maya is described as the illusory energy that covers our true understanding and binds us to the material world. It creates a sense of duality, causing us to perceive ourselves as separate from the Supreme Being and identifying with our temporary material bodies.

2. Origin of Maya: Maya is an energy emanating from the Supreme Being. In the Gita, Krishna explains that He is the source of both the material and spiritual worlds and

that Maya is one of His divine energies.

3. Effects of Maya: Maya leads to ignorance and attachment to the material world. It deludes us into identifying with our temporary bodies, causing suffering and entangling us in the cycle of birth and death. It creates a false sense of happiness derived from material possessions and sensory experiences.

4. Overcoming Maya: The Gita provides various methods to overcome Maya and attain liberation (moksha):

    a. Knowledge: Acquiring spiritual knowledge and understanding the true nature of the self and the Supreme Being helps in overcoming Maya. By realizing our eternal spiritual essence and the temporary nature of the material world, we can transcend Maya's influence.
    b. Devotional Service: Engaging in devotional service (bhakti yoga) is emphasized as a powerful means to transcend Maya. By cultivating a loving relationship with the Supreme through acts of devotion, such as prayer, meditation, chanting, and serving others selflessly, one can gradually rise above the illusionary energy of Maya.
    c. Renunciation: The Gita also discusses the practice of renunciation (sannyasa) as a means to overcome Maya. This involves detachment from material possessions, desires, and outcomes, focusing on selfless service and surrendering the fruits of one's actions to the Supreme.

d. Discerning the Real from the Unreal: Developing discrimination (viveka) between the eternal spiritual reality and the temporary material world is essential to overcome Maya. By recognizing the impermanence and illusory nature of the material realm, one can cultivate detachment and a deeper connection with the spiritual essence.
e. Divine Grace: The Gita emphasizes the importance of divine grace in overcoming Maya. It teaches that through surrendering to the Supreme Being, seeking His guidance and protection, and relying on His mercy, one can transcend the influence of Maya.

The teachings of the Bhagavad Gita encourage individuals to strive for spiritual knowledge, engage in devotional practices, cultivate detachment, discern the real from the unreal, and seek divine grace to overcome Maya and attain liberation from the material world.

A person who has overcome Maya possesses certain characteristics. These traits reflect their spiritual growth and liberation from the influence of Maya. Here are some characteristics of such an individual:

1. Awareness of the Self: A person who has overcome Maya has a deep understanding of their true spiritual nature. They recognize themselves as eternal souls, distinct from their temporary material bodies. They have realized the divine essence within themselves and in all beings.

2. Detachment: Such an individual is detached from the ma-

terial world and its attractions. They are not swayed by the illusion of temporary pleasures and possessions. They do not crave material success or recognition, understanding the impermanence of worldly achievements.

3. Equanimity: One who has transcended Maya maintains equanimity in the face of life's dualities. They are unaffected by success or failure, joy or sorrow. They understand the transient nature of these experiences and remain rooted in inner peace and spiritual stability.

4. Selflessness and Compassion: Having risen above the illusion of separateness, a person who has overcome Maya is filled with genuine compassion for all living beings. They selflessly serve others and actively work towards alleviating suffering in the world.

5. Knowledge and Wisdom: Such individuals have acquired spiritual knowledge and wisdom, enabling them to discern the real from the unreal. They possess deep insights into the nature of existence and the workings of divine energy. Their wisdom guides their actions and choices.

6. Humility: Despite their spiritual advancement, those who have transcended Maya remain humble and free from ego. They recognize the Supreme Being's grace and acknowledge that all achievements are due to divine blessings. They treat all beings with respect and humility.

7. Unwavering Devotion: A person who has overcome Maya is devoted to the Supreme with unwavering faith. They engage in devotional practices with love and sincerity, of-

fering their actions, thoughts, and emotions to the divine. Their devotion fuels their spiritual journey.

8. Freedom from Fear: Having transcended Maya, they are free from the fear of birth, death, and the material world's uncertainties. They understand the eternal nature of the soul and the ultimate goal of union with the Supreme. Their trust in the divine provides them with inner strength and fearlessness.

These characteristics reflect the transformation and liberation that occur when one transcends Maya. However, it's important to note that the journey of spiritual growth is ongoing, and individuals may exhibit these characteristics to varying degrees based on their progress and personal experiences.

Overcoming Maya

Amidst the dance of life's illusory play,
A universal power, Maya weaves its art,
Concealing truth, leading our souls astray,
Binding us tight, keeping us far apart.

In Maya's grip, we see the world askew,
A veil of ignorance upon our eyes,
Attachments formed, desires ever grew,
Lost in the realm where ego amplifies.

In darkest night, light does gleam,
Gita's wisdom to pierce through Maya's guise,
Knowledge unveiled, like a sacred stream,
Awakening souls to see through tempting lies.

Through devotion's flame, Maya dissipates,
Liberation beckons, freedom awaits.

With knowledge as our shield, we break the chains,
Discerning truth from transient illusion,
Bhakti's fire within our hearts sustains,
Unveiling depths of divine delusion.

Renunciation, a pathway to embrace,
Detaching from the fruits of our actions,
In surrender, finding eternal grace,
As Maya's hold dissolves, satisfaction.

Maya dance fades, revealing blazing light,
The eternal essence of our true self,
With every step, we soar to boundless height,
Transcending Maya's grip, transcending ego self.

Oh, Lord's teachings, beacon in the night,
Guide us, inspire us, toward inner light.

Control the Mind

While the Gita offers guidance on controlling the mind, it does not provide explicit techniques for mind control in the sense of manipulating or dominating others. Instead, it focuses on self-discipline and achieving mastery over one's own mind. Here are some key teachings from the Gita that can be applied to develop control over the mind:

1. Self-awareness: Lord Krishna emphasizes the importance of self-awareness and understanding the nature of the mind. By observing and becoming aware of our thoughts, emotions, and desires, we can gain insight into the workings of the mind and begin to exert control over it.

   From wherever the mind wanders due to its flickering and unsteady nature, one must certainly withdraw it and bring it back under the control of the self. (Gita 6.26)

2. Discipline and restraint: He encourages the practice of self-discipline and restraint as essential means to control the mind. It emphasizes the need to curb excessive desires, attachments, and impulsive actions, which can disturb the mind's equilibrium.

   One must deliver oneself with the help of one's own mind, and not degrade oneself. The mind is the friend of the conditioned soul, and his enemy as well." (Gita 6.5)

3. Meditation and contemplation: The Gita advocates the practice of meditation and contemplation as powerful

tools for controlling the mind. By focusing the mind on a single point, such as a mantra, the breath, or an object of concentration, one can gradually calm the mind and gain greater control over its fluctuating nature.

When meditation is mastered, the mind is unwavering like the flame of a lamp in a windless place." (6.19)

4. Detachment: The Gita teaches the importance of cultivating detachment from the fruits of one's actions. By performing actions without attachment to the outcomes, one can reduce the influence of desires and cravings on the mind, leading to greater mental clarity and control.
5. Yoga: The Gita presents various paths of yoga, including Karma Yoga (the path of selfless action), Bhakti Yoga (the path of devotion), and Jnana Yoga (the path of knowledge). These paths provide practical methods for purifying the mind, cultivating virtues, and attaining control over one's thoughts and emotions.

The Gita's teachings on mind control are primarily focused on personal development, self-mastery, and spiritual growth. The ethical principles and practices outlined in the Gita aim to align the mind with higher ideals and virtues, rather than seeking to manipulate or control others.

The key benefits of mind control as elucidated in the Gita are:

1. Clarity and focus: By developing control over the mind, one can achieve clarity and focus on one's thoughts and actions. A controlled mind is less prone to distractions and can concentrate on the task at hand. This enables indi-

viduals to make better decisions, enhance their productivity, and achieve their goals more effectively.

2. Emotional stability: The mind often fluctuates due to the influence of emotions such as anger, fear, and desire. Through mind control practices, one can gain mastery over these emotions and achieve emotional stability. This allows individuals to respond to challenging situations with equanimity, reducing stress and enhancing overall well-being.

   The uncontrolled mind does not guess that the Atman is present. How can it meditate? Without meditation, where is peace? Without peace, where is happiness?" (Gita 2.66)

3. Self-discipline: Mind control involves cultivating self-discipline, which is essential for personal growth and spiritual development. By restraining impulsive actions and desires, individuals can strengthen their willpower and develop a greater sense of self-control. This promotes a disciplined lifestyle and helps overcome negative habits and addictions.

4. Enhanced decision-making: A controlled mind enables individuals to make rational and wise decisions. When the mind is free from turbulence and emotional biases, it can evaluate situations objectively, consider different perspectives, and make choices that align with one's values and goals.

5. Spiritual growth: The Gita views mind control to attain spiritual growth and self-realization. By gaining mastery

over the mind, one can transcend the limitations of the ego and connect with their true nature. This paves the way for spiritual awakening and the realization of the eternal Self.

A person is said to have achieved yoga, the union with the Self, when the perfectly disciplined mind gets freedom from all desires and becomes absorbed in the Self alone. (Gita 6.18)

6. Inner peace and happiness: Mind control practices lead to inner peace and lasting happiness. When the mind is no longer swayed by external circumstances or the fluctuations of desires, it becomes anchored in a state of equanimity and contentment. This inner peace remains unshaken even amidst life's challenges, fostering a sense of fulfillment and joy.

   For one who has conquered the mind, the mind is the best of friends; but for one who has failed to do so, the mind will remain the greatest enemy. (Gita 6.6)

The significance of gaining control over the mind is not only for spiritual growth but for personal well-being, inner peace as well.

Mind Control

Where thoughts roam, untamed and free,
A guide to rein in their wild spree.
Meditation calms the mind's commotion,
A rhythmic breath, a soothing devotion.

In discipline and will, serenity is sought,
A refuge where mental clarity is taught.
No longer captive to desires allure,
The mind becomes master, steady and sure.

Embrace the Lord's poetic sway,
A sanctuary where wisdom holds sway.
With guidance, thoughts find their place,
Peaceful tranquility blooms, a gentle grace.

The Ultimate Reality - Brahman

The concept of Brahman in the Bhagavad Gita is a profound and central idea in Hindu philosophy. Brahman refers to the ultimate, supreme, and unchanging reality that underlies and pervades the entire universe. It is often described as the absolute, infinite, and eternal essence that transcends all limitations of time, space, and causation.

In the Gita, Brahman is presented as the underlying essence of all beings, the source of all existence, and the goal of spiritual realization. It is depicted as the divine, cosmic consciousness that permeates everything in creation. Krishna, who serves as the guide and teacher in the Gita, reveals his identity as an incarnation of Brahman.

Brahman is characterized as being beyond the physical and material world, beyond the dualities of good and evil, pleasure and pain, and beyond all forms of human comprehension. It is described as the substratum of the universe, the essence from which all things arise and to which all things return.

The Gita emphasizes that realizing one's true nature as Brahman is the highest spiritual attainment. It teaches that all beings are essentially divine and interconnected with Brahman. The path to realizing this divine nature is through self-realization, inner awakening, and union with the divine.

Krishna explains various paths to attain this realization, such as the path of selfless action (Karma Yoga), the path of devotion and love (Bhakti Yoga), the path of knowledge and wisdom (Jnana

Yoga), and the path of meditation and contemplation (Dhyana Yoga). These paths are meant to lead individuals to a direct experience and realization of their unity with Brahman.

In summary, the concept of Brahman in the Bhagavad Gita represents the ultimate reality, the supreme consciousness that underlies the universe. It is the goal of spiritual realization and the source from which all beings arise. Understanding and realizing one's unity with Brahman is considered the highest state of enlightenment and liberation.

Here are a few verses from the Bhagavad Gita that discuss the concept of Brahman:

1. Chapter 8, Verse 3:

   The Supreme Personality of Godhead said: The indestructible, transcendental living entity is called Brahman, and his eternal nature is called the self. Action pertaining to the development of these material bodies is called karma, or fruitive activities.

2. Chapter 9, Verse 22:

   To those who are constantly devoted and who engage in the service of the Supreme with love, the Supreme Lord gives the understanding by which they can come to Him. Brahman, Paramatma, and Bhagavan are three features of the same Supreme Personality of Godhead.

3. Chapter 10, Verse 8:

   I am the source of all spiritual and material worlds. Everything emanates from Me. The wise who know this perfectly engage in My devotional service and worship Me with all their hearts."

4. Chapter 14, Verse 27:

   For one who has taken his birth, death is certain; and for one who is dead, birth is certain. Therefore, in the unavoidable discharge of your duty, you should not lament."

5. Chapter 15, Verse 16:

   There are two classes of beings, the fallible and the infallible. In the material world, every living entity is fallible, and in the spiritual world every living entity is called infallible."

These verses offer insights into the nature of Brahman, its relationship with the Supreme Personality of Godhead, and the understanding of the eternal soul.

In Chapter 13, Lord Krishna enlightens Arjuna about two essential aspects: the body (material nature) and the soul (spiritual nature). He explains that the body is perishable and subject to constant change, while the soul is eternal and immutable.

Krishna describes the body as made up of the physical elements, the senses, the mind, and intelligence. He emphasizes that the body should not be identified as its true self but recognized as a temporary vessel.

He then introduces the concept of the field (kshetra) and the knower of the field (kshetrajna). The body is referred to as the field, and the soul, which is the conscious being residing within the body, is the knower of the field. The knower of the field is the true self, distinct from the body.

Krishna explains that the true self, the knower of the field, is also present in all beings, permeating the entire universe. This eternal self is often referred to as the Brahman. He further explains that the knowledge of the field and the knower of the field is considered true knowledge.

The Lord elaborates on the qualities of the knower of the field, describing it as the witness, the sustainer, the enjoyer, and the supreme controller. He clarifies that the individual souls, although part of the Supreme Brahman, are distinct entities with their own identities.

Krishna emphasizes that understanding the difference between the body and the soul, and recognizing the eternal nature of the soul, leads to liberation and self-realization. He advises Arjuna to cultivate knowledge, detachment, and the ability to discern between the temporary and the eternal.

The chapter concludes with Krishna encouraging Arjuna to constantly reflect upon the teachings and to meditate on the Supreme to attain liberation from the cycle of birth and death.

Chapter 13 of the Gita highlights the distinction between the perishable body and the eternal soul, referred to as the knower of the field or Brahman. Recognizing the true self as distinct from the body and cultivating spiritual knowledge and detachment are emphasized as essential steps on the path to liberation and self-realization.

The Tapestry of Life

Brahman, the essence, vast and all-pervading,
Infinite, eternal, that source never fading.
The cosmic consciousness, the ultimate truth,
From which all creation, springs forth, in sooth.

Iswara, the Lord, with benevolent grace,
Presides overall, in every time and space.
The divine embodiment, the guiding light,
Dispelling ignorance, unveiling wisdom's sight.

Soul, the divine spark, within mortal guise,
A fragment of Brahman, that never dies.
Through countless lives, it journeys on the way,
Seeking reunion, with the eternal ray.

Atman, the true self, transcending the strife,
Infinite, unchanging, eternal life.

Beyond the transient, it finds its true home,
Realizing unity, no longer to roam.

Brahman, Iswara, soul, and Atman, entwined,
The tapestry of existence, divinely designed.
In sacred union, they dance, and they weave,
A symphony of oneness, in which we believe.

In realms divine, a tale unfolds, untold,
Of Brahman, Iswara, soul, and Atman's hold.
Brahman, the essence, all-encompassing, vast,
Eternal truth, from which creation is cast.

Iswara, the guiding Lord, with grace divine,
Presides overall, with love that brightly shines.
In wisdom's light, ignorance is dispelled,
Revealing the path where truth is upheld.

Soul, a spark divine, within mortal frame,
Fragment of Brahman, seeking reunion's claim.

Through countless lives, it wanders and explores,
Longing for unity, where its essence soars.

Atman, the true self, beyond transient days,
Unchanging, infinite, in eternal ways.
In realms beyond, its true nature unfurled,
Realizing unity, no longer in the world.

Brahman, Iswara, soul, and Atman's embrace,
A tapestry of existence, woven with grace.
In sacred union, they dance and entwine,
Revealing the truth, where divine light will shine.

In the realm of eternal truth, a tale unfolds,
Of Brahman, the boundless, where all wisdom molds.
Iswara, the guiding force, with loving embrace,
Leading seekers on the path, to divine grace.

Soul, a divine spark, in mortal body resides,
Yearning for union with the infinite tides.

Fragment of Brahman, it traverses the spheres,
Seeking liberation, transcending earthly fears.

Atman, the true self, beyond the transient veil,
Immersed in divine essence, it will never fail.
Unchanging, eternal, connected to the divine,
Realizing its oneness, in the sacred shrine.

Brahman, the ultimate reality, expansive and vast,
Beyond comprehension, a divine contrast.
Iswara, the embodiment, the divine supreme,
Guiding souls to liberation, like a sacred dream.

Soul, an individual expression, seeking its way,
Through the cycle of birth and death, it may stray.
Yet bound to Brahman, its ultimate destination,
To merge in divine unity, in realization.

Atman, the essence within, the true divine core,
Shining brightly, forever and ever more.

Infinite and eternal, it seeks its divine source,
Transcending limitations, on its destined course.

Brahman, Iswara, soul, and Atman's embrace,
A tapestry of existence, interconnected in space.
Unveiling the cosmic dance, the divine play,
Revealing the eternal truth, through every day.

Unity In Diversity

The concepts of the unity of all beings and the reality of the material world can indeed be reconciled in the teachings of the Bhagavad Gita, a sacred Hindu scripture. The Gita provides a philosophical framework that explores the nature of reality, the relationship between the material and spiritual aspects of existence, and the unity underlying all beings.

According to the Gita, at the fundamental level, there is a unity that pervades all of creation. This unity is often referred to as the Atman, the eternal and unchanging essence or self that is present in all living beings. The Gita teaches that this Atman is not separate from the ultimate reality known as Brahman, which is the supreme consciousness or divine principle that underlies the universe.

However, the Gita also acknowledges the existence of the material world and recognizes that we live in a realm of duality, where we experience various forms, objects, and relationships. It recognizes that the material world is subject to change, impermanence, and suffering. The Gita does not deny the reality of the material world but provides a perspective on how to navigate it while realizing our spiritual nature.

The Gita teaches that while the material world is transient, our true nature is spiritual and eternal. It emphasizes the importance of understanding the impermanence of the material realm and cultivating detachment from its fleeting nature. By recognizing the temporary nature of the material world, one can shift their focus from material pursuits and instead seek a deeper connection with the eternal and spiritual reality.

The Gita encourages individuals to perform their duties and responsibilities in the world with a sense of detachment and selflessness, without being overly attached to the outcomes or rewards of their actions. It teaches that by acting selflessly, performing one's duties with devotion and without attachment, one can attain a state of equanimity and spiritual realization.

In this way, the Gita reconciles the unity of all beings with the reality of the material world by guiding individuals to recognize the underlying unity while navigating the experiences of the material realm with detachment and spiritual awareness. It teaches that by realizing our true nature as spiritual beings and living in harmony with the unity that pervades all of creation, we can find lasting peace, fulfillment, and transcendence beyond the transient nature of the material world.

The dual nature of the Divine Being, as understood in the Bhagavad Gita, is an important aspect of its teachings. The Gita presents the Divine Being as both immanent and transcendent, embodying both the material and spiritual dimensions of existence.

On one hand, the Gita describes the Divine Being as transcendent, beyond the material world and its limitations. It refers to this aspect as the Supreme Reality or Brahman, which is the ultimate source of all creation, the unchanging and eternal essence that underlies the universe. This aspect of the Divine Being represents transcendent nature, which is beyond the grasp of ordinary human perception and understanding.

On the other hand, the Gita also teaches that the Divine Being is immanent, pervading all aspects of creation, including the material world and all living beings. It presents the concept of Ishvara, which refers to the divine manifestation or the personal aspect of the Divine Being. Ishvara represents the immanent nature of the Divine, actively involved in the affairs of the world and the lives of individuals.

The Gita suggests that although the Divine Being is beyond the material realm, it chooses to manifest itself in various forms and ways to guide and support sentient beings. This dual nature of the Divine reflects the understanding that the Supreme Reality not only transcends the material world but also permeates and sustains it.

In the context of unity and the reality of the material world, the dual nature of the Divine Being serves as a unifying concept. The Gita teaches that the same Divine Being, which is both transcendent and immanent, dwells within all living beings as the Atman—the individual soul or self. This recognition of the divinity within oneself and all beings forms the basis for understanding the unity that exists despite the diversity of forms and experiences in the material world.

By realizing the immanent aspect of the Divine within oneself and others, the Gita teaches that one can cultivate a sense of oneness, compassion, and love for all beings. This understanding helps bridge the gap between the material and spiritual realms, bringing harmony and a deeper realization of the unity that underlies all existence.

In summary, the dual nature of the Divine Being in the Bhagavad Gita, as both transcendent and immanent, helps reconcile the unity of all beings with the reality of the material world. It emphasizes the presence of the divine within oneself and others, enabling a recognition of unity beyond the apparent diversity and transient nature of the material realm.

Here are a few verses from the Bhagavad Gita that exemplify the concepts of the unity of all beings and the dual nature of the Divine Being:

1. Unity of all beings:

   Who sees Me everywhere and sees everything in Me, he never becomes separated from Me, nor do I become separated from him. (6:32)

   To those who are constantly devoted and who worship Me with love, I give the understanding by which they can come to Me. (9:22)

2. Immanent and transcendent nature of the Divine Being:

   I am the Self, O Gudakesha, seated in the hearts of all creatures. I am the beginning, the middle, and the end of all beings. (10:20)

   There is nothing higher than Me. All this is strung on Me as pearls are strung on a thread. (7:7)

3. Recognition of the divinity within oneself and all beings:

   He who sees the Supreme Lord dwelling alike in all beings, the Imperishable amidst the perishable, truly sees.

> (13:27)
>
> The Lord resides in the hearts of all creatures, O Arjuna, and directs the wanderings of all living entities, who are seated as on a machine, made of material energy. (18:61)

The verses above highlight the teachings of the Gita regarding the unity of all beings, the immanent and transcendent nature of the Divine Being, and the recognition of divinity within oneself and others. They provide a glimpse into the profound spiritual wisdom and guidance offered by the Gita on these topics.

Unity in Diversity

In unity's embrace, the Gita speaks,
Revealing truth that every soul can seek.
Dual nature of the Divine unfolds,
Immanent and transcendent, as it holds.

The Atman, essence pure, unchanging, free,
The divine spark within, all hearts can see.
Brahman, supreme reality's domain,
Beyond the grasp of mortal minds, remain.

Yet in this vast expanse, the Divine dwells,
Within each being, its presence gently tells.
Ishvara, personal aspect, near and far,
Guides, sustains, and lights life's wondrous star.

Through verses sung, the Gita's wisdom weaves,
Unity in diversity it conceives.
Within all souls, the sacred truth resides,
Connecting threads of love that gently guides.

So let us seek the unity divine,
In every heart, let compassion shine.
For in this dance of life, we shall find,
The truth that unites, and sets souls aligned.

Self and Buddhi

Here are a few key points and supporting verses from the Gita that offers teachings about the Self:

1. The eternal nature of the self that transcends birth and death:

   Never was there a time when I did not exist, nor you, nor all these kings; nor in the future shall any of us cease to be." (2.12)

2. The distinction between the body and the self:

   Just as a person puts on new garments, giving up old ones, similarly, the soul accepts new material bodies, giving up the old and useless ones." (2.22)

3. The indestructibility of the self that is beyond the reach of external forces:

   Weapons cannot cut it, fire cannot burn it, water cannot wet it, and the wind cannot dry it." (2.23)

4. The immutability of the self:

   The soul is never born and never dies; it is not slain when the body is slain." (2.20)

5. The self as the witness and experiencer – it is the unchanging witness behind all experiences, beyond the realm of perception, and distinct from the transient physical body

It is said that the soul is invisible, inconceivable, and immutable. Knowing this, you should not grieve for the body." (2.25)

6. The interconnectedness of all selves - the enlightened ones perceive the underlying unity of all beings, recognizing the same divine essence within everyone, regardless of their outer differences.

   The humble sages, by virtue of true knowledge, see with equal vision a learned and gentle brahmana, a cow, an elephant, a dog, and a dog-eater." (5.18)

These verses from the Gita provide insights into the teachings about the self, highlighting its eternal, indestructible, immutable, and interconnected nature. The Gita encourages individuals to recognize the true self beyond the transient physical body and to cultivate self-realization and spiritual growth.

In the context of the Gita, the terms "soul" and "self" are often used interchangeably to refer to the individual essence or Atman. Both terms denote the eternal, conscious aspect of a being that is distinct from the physical body. The soul/self is the unchanging witness and experiencer of life, unaffected by the fluctuations of the material world.

The Gita teaches that the self/soul is eternal, indestructible, and immutable, while the physical body is temporary and subject to birth and death. The self is seen as the essence that transcends the body and continues its existence even after the death of the physical form. Therefore, in the context of the Bhagavad Gita, the soul and the self are generally understood to be the same, referring to the eternal aspect of an individual beyond the material body.

In the Gita, Buddhi refers to the intellect or the faculty of discernment. It is the higher aspect of the mind that allows one to make decisions, discriminate between right and wrong, and understand deeper truths. The Gita explores the connection between the self (Atman) and Buddhi in the context of spiritual growth and self-realization. Here are a few key points regarding their connection:

1. Buddhi as a tool for self-realization:

   The Gita teaches that Buddhi plays a crucial role in attaining self-realization. By cultivating a discerning intellect, one can distinguish between the eternal self and the transient material world. Through Buddhi, one can discern their true nature and align their actions with spiritual principles.

2. Buddhi as the guide to right action:

   The Gita emphasizes the importance of Buddhi in making informed choices and acting in accordance with dharma (righteousness). Buddhi helps one understand the consequences of their actions and make decisions that are aligned with higher principles and moral values.

3. Buddhi as the bridge between the self and the senses:

   The senses and the mind have a tendency to be influenced by desires, attachments, and external stimuli. Buddhi acts as a bridge between the self and the senses, allowing one to exercise control over their thoughts, emotions, and actions. It helps in directing the senses towards the pursuit of spiritual growth and aligning them with the higher self.

4. Developing a purified Buddhi:

   The Gita encourages individuals to purify their Buddhi through spiritual practices such as self-discipline, self-reflection, meditation, and seeking knowledge from spiritual texts and enlightened teachers. A purified Buddhi becomes a clear channel for the self to express itself and guides one towards self-realization.

Overall, the Gita portrays Buddhi as a vital instrument in the journey of self-discovery and spiritual evolution. By cultivating a discerning intellect and aligning it with the eternal self, individuals can attain self-realization and experience a deeper connection with their true nature.

Buddhi Guide

Within the depths where consciousness resides,
A flame ablaze, the self's eternal light.
Buddhi, the guide, discerns truth's subtle tides,
Through intellect, it steers the soul aright.

A beacon bright, amid life's shifting sea,
Buddhi unveils the path of righteous choice.
With wisdom's touch, it sets the spirit free,
And lends a steady, clear, discerning voice.

Through senses' sway, distractions may arise,
But Buddhi's reign brings clarity of thought.
It sees beyond the veil of ego's guise,
Revealing self, the essence that's unsought.

In harmony, the self and Buddhi dance,
A symphony of truth, both intertwined.
Awakening the soul's innate expanse,
Together, in unity, they're aligned.

So seek within, the self and Buddhi's grace,
Embrace their gifts, their wisdom, and their might.
Unveil the truth, the boundless inner space,
And journey towards self's radiant light.

Devotion and non-attachment

In the Gita, the role of devotion (bhakti) is emphasized as a powerful path to spiritual development. Devotion is regarded as a fundamental aspect of one's relationship with the divine, leading to a deeper understanding of the self and a profound connection with the Supreme Being. Through devotion, individuals cultivate love, surrender, and single-minded focus on the divine, transcending the limitations of the ego and attaining spiritual growth.

The Bhagavad Gita describes various forms of devotion, including devotion through action (karma yoga), devotion through knowledge (jnana yoga), and devotion through love and surrender (bhakti yoga). Bhakti yoga, specifically, emphasizes the practice of devotion and love towards God as the primary means of spiritual realization. It encourages individuals to develop a personal relationship with the divine, characterized by love, reverence, and unwavering faith.

To illustrate the role of devotion, let's consider a verse from the Bhagavad Gita (Chapter 9, Verse 22):

"To those who are constantly devoted and who engage in worshipping Me with love, I give the understanding by which they can come to Me."

This verse emphasizes that those who maintain unwavering devotion and offer their worship with love and reverence are blessed with divine guidance and understanding. It suggests that through devotion, individuals develop a deep connection with the Supreme Being, and in turn, the divine reveals the path to reach the ultimate goal of union with God.

Devotion is not limited to mere rituals or external practices but involves a genuine, heartfelt longing for the divine. It is about cultivating a deep love and surrender towards God, recognizing the divine presence within oneself and all beings. Devotion transcends religious boundaries and is open to people of different backgrounds, as it is based on the universal principle of love and devotion towards the divine.

Another verse that highlights the significance of devotion is from Chapter 18, Verse 65:

"Fix your mind on Me, be devoted to Me, offer service to Me, bow down to Me, and you shall certainly reach Me. I promise you because you are very dear to Me."

Here, Lord Krishna, the divine teacher in the Bhagavad Gita, emphasizes the importance of directing one's mind and heart towards the divine. The verse emphasizes devotion as a means to attain the ultimate union with God. By offering one's thoughts, actions, and service to God, and surrendering the ego, individuals can experience the divine presence and ultimately merge with the Supreme.

Devotion in the Bhagavad Gita is not limited to a particular religious practice or belief system. It is an invitation to cultivate a personal and loving relationship with the divine, regardless of one's background or religious affiliation. It is a path of deep connection, love, and surrender, allowing individuals to transcend the limitations of the ego and experience spiritual growth and fulfillment.

The Gita teaches that devotion (bhakti) plays a significant role in spiritual development. Through unwavering love, surrender, and single-minded focus on the divine, individuals cultivate a deep connection with the Supreme Being. Devotion leads to a profound understanding of the self, divine guidance, and the ultimate realization of union with God - il highlighting its transformative power in the journey of spiritual growth and self-realization.

Let's explore further the role of devotion on the path of spiritual development:

1. Uniting with the Divine:

   I am the Self, O Gudakesha, seated in the hearts of all creatures. I am the beginning, the middle and the end of all beings. (10:20)
   The presence of the divine is within all beings. By cultivating devotion, individuals can recognize and unite with the divine essence that resides within themselves and all of creation.

   Devotion in the Gita is portrayed as a path of surrender and love that leads to the union with the divine. Through heartfelt devotion, individuals develop a deep connection with God and experience the divine presence within themselves and all of creation. This union is depicted as the goal of spiritual development, where the individual realizes their true nature and merges with the Supreme.

2. Overcoming the Ego:

   He who is not hateful towards any creature, friendly and

compassionate, free from possessiveness and egoism, balanced in pleasure and pain, forgiving, ever-content, steady in meditation, self-controlled, and possessed of firm conviction, with mind and intellect dedicated to Me, such a devotee of Mine is dear to Me. (12:13)

The qualities of a devoted individual who has transcended the ego and developed virtues such as compassion, selflessness, and self-control is dear to the divine.

Devotion serves as a means to transcend the limitations of the ego, which is often associated with attachment, desires, and a sense of separateness. By cultivating devotion, individuals redirect their focus from the ego-driven desires towards selfless love and service to the divine. This shift in consciousness allows them to break free from the clutches of the ego and experience a state of unity and oneness with the divine.

3. Transforming Actions:

   Whatever you do, whatever you eat, whatever you offer in sacrifice, whatever you give, whatever you practice as austerity, O son of Kunti, do it as an offering to Me. (9:27)

   This verse encourages individuals to offer their actions, whether it be work, food, sacrifice, charity, or spiritual practices, as an offering to God. By dedicating their actions to the divine, individuals transform ordinary actions into acts of devotion and service.

Devotion also transforms one's actions by infusing them with love and a sense of divine service. We are encouraged to offer our actions to God, recognizing that all actions can be an expression of devotion when performed with the right intention. By engaging in selfless service and dedicating the results of their actions to the divine, individuals purify their minds and hearts, leading to spiritual growth and development.

4. Bhakti Yoga:

   To those who are constantly devoted and who engage in worshipping Me with love, I give the understanding by which they can come to Me. (9:22)

   Through the power of devotion and love towards God through unwavering devotion, one develops a deep understanding and realization of the divine, leading them to the path of union with God.

   Bhakti yoga is a specific path of devotion outlined in the Gita. It emphasizes cultivating love, surrender, and devotion towards God as the primary means of attaining spiritual realization. Bhakti yoga involves various practices such as chanting the divine names, singing hymns of praise, studying sacred texts, and engaging in devotional rituals. These practices deepen the individual's connection with the divine and nurture a profound love and longing for God.

5. Grace and Divine Guidance:

   To those who are constantly devoted and who are always engaged in serving Me with love, I give the understanding by which they can come to Me. (10:10)

   This verse reiterates that through unwavering devotion and selfless service, individuals are bestowed with divine understanding and guidance, helping them progress on their spiritual path.

   Devotion opens the door to divine grace and guidance - those who sincerely devote themselves to God are bestowed with divine blessings and assistance. The Supreme Being, out of love for the devotee, offers guidance, protection, and spiritual wisdom to help them progress on their path. Devotion establishes a reciprocal relationship between the individual and the divine, where the devotee's love and surrender are met with divine support and grace.

6. Universal Nature of Devotion:

   To those who are constantly devoted and who engage in worshipping Me with love, I give the understanding by which they can come to Me. (9:22)

   Devotion is not limited to a particular religious practice but is open to all who engage in worshipping the divine with love and devotion. It emphasizes the universal nature of devotion and the inclusiveness of the path.

> Devotion is based on the principle of love and reverence towards the Supreme, and it transcends religious boundaries, inviting all to connect with the divine in their own unique way. Devotion is a path of love, surrender, and selfless service, leading to spiritual growth, divine grace, and the ultimate realization of one's true nature.

In the teachings of the Bhagavad Gita, devotion (bhakti) and non-attachment (vairagya) are interconnected and mutually supportive aspects of spiritual development. While they may seem to be contradictory at first glance, they are two sides of the same coin, working together to deepen one's spiritual journey.

Devotion involves cultivating a deep love, reverence, and surrender towards the divine. It is about developing a personal relationship with God, recognizing the divine presence within oneself and all beings. Devotion requires a wholehearted and unwavering commitment to the divine, with a focus on love and service.

Non-attachment, on the other hand, refers to a state of inner detachment from the fruits of one's actions and the transient nature of the material world. It is the ability to remain unaffected by the outcomes of one's actions, desires, and attachments. Non-attachment does not imply a lack of care or indifference but rather an understanding that true fulfillment and liberation come from transcending worldly attachments.

The relationship between devotion and non-attachment can be understood as follows:

1. Non-attachment as a Tool for Devotion:

You have the right to perform your prescribed duty, but you are not entitled to the fruits of your actions. Never consider yourself the cause of the results of your activities, and never be attached to not doing your duty. (2:47) By cultivating non-attachment, individuals can focus on their actions as acts of devotion, offering them to the divine without being attached to personal desires or expectations.

Non-attachment serves as a tool to deepen one's devotion. By cultivating non-attachment, individuals develop the ability to detach from the outcomes of their actions, relinquish the ego's control, and surrender to the divine will. This allows them to offer their actions, thoughts, and emotions as acts of devotion without being consumed by personal desires or expectations.

2. Devotion as a means to Non-attachment:

Devotion, in turn, supports the development of non-attachment. Through a deep connection with the divine, individuals realize the impermanence and transient nature of the material world. This realization helps them detach from the ephemeral and focus on the eternal and spiritual aspects of life. Devotion nurtures a sense of inner contentment and fulfillment that transcends external attachments, leading to a state of non-attachment.

Always absorbed in the Self, taking refuge in solitude, with a controlled mind and body, free from possessions and craving for possessions, one should constantly try to practice meditation and attain peace. (12:14)

By absorbing oneself in the divine, seeking solitude, and cultivating a controlled mind and body. Through devotion, individuals develop a detachment from possessions and cravings, focusing on the eternal and spiritual aspects of life.

3. Harmonious Balance:

Perform your duty in equipoise, O Arjuna, abandoning all attachment to success or failure. Such equanimity is called yoga. (2:48)

An essential part of spiritual practice is performing one's duty with equanimity, abandoning attachment to success or failure - maintaining a balanced approach, free from attachment.

Devotion and non-attachment work in harmony to create a balanced spiritual approach. While devotion involves love, surrender, and attachment to the divine, non-attachment ensures that this attachment does not become a source of suffering or hinder spiritual progress. Non-attachment helps individuals maintain equanimity in the face of challenges, not being swayed by temporary circumstances or external influences.

4. Freedom and Liberation:

The embodied soul may be restricted from sense enjoyment, though the taste for sense objects remains. But,

> ceasing such engagements by experiencing a higher taste, he is fixed in consciousness. (2:59)
>
> Individuals may have desires and attachments, but by experiencing a higher consciousness through spiritual practices, they can transcend the pull of sensory enjoyments. Through devotion and non-attachment, one becomes established in higher states of consciousness.
>
> The ultimate goal of both devotion and non-attachment is spiritual freedom and liberation. Devotion allows individuals to experience a deep union with the divine, while non-attachment liberates them from the bondage of desires and attachments. Together, they lead to the realization of one's true nature and the attainment of spiritual liberation.

In summary, devotion and non-attachment are not conflicting but complementary aspects of the spiritual path. Devotion cultivates love, surrender, and a deep connection with the divine, while non-attachment fosters detachment from transient desires and outcomes. Together, they create a balanced approach, leading to spiritual growth, inner freedom, and the realization of one's true nature.

Non-Attachment supports Devotion

In divine absorption, a higher path receive,
With love and surrender, where souls believe,
In devotion's embrace, spirit hearts intertwines,
With non-attachment's light, divine and sublime.

In temples adorned with incense's sweet scent,
Devotees gather, their spirits content,
Their voices united in hymns of devotion,
Seeking the path to eternal liberation.

With eyes filled with longing, they bow and they pray,
In humble surrender, they find their own way,
Their hearts overflowing with love for the divine,
In devotion's embrace, their souls brightly shine.

Yet amidst their ardor, a truth they hold dear,
Non-attachment whispers, dispelling all fear,
For in the pursuit of devotion's pure flame,
Detachment from outcomes brings freedom's true aim.

They offer their actions, selflessly, with grace,
Knowing the fruits belong to the eternal space,
Their devotion unblemished by ego's demand,
They hold steadfast, guided by non-attachment's hand.

In triumph or failure, they stand undisturbed,
Neither praise nor censure leaves their hearts perturbed,
Their focus on service, with love they bestow,
Non-attachment's wisdom their actions do show.

With devotion's fire and non-attachment's might,
They traverse the path, radiant with inner light,
For in the union of both, they find the key,
To liberation's shores, where souls wander free.

Devotion and non-attachment, intertwined,
In this ballad's verses, their essence defined,
May we too embrace them, with hearts open wide,
In devotion's fervor, with non-attachment's guide.

The Battle of Life

The concept of life as a battlefield is prominently discussed in the Gita which portrays life as a constant struggle, where individuals face various challenges and conflicts both internally and externally.

A few verses that exemplify the idea of life as a battlefield:

> Arjuna, behold this great army of yours, arrayed by the sons of Pandu, skillfully marshaled by your able disciple, the son of Drupada. (1:2)

This verse sets the stage for the conversation between Lord Krishna and the warrior Arjuna on the battlefield of Kurukshetra. The army represents the challenges and adversities that one encounters in life. It symbolizes the multitude of forces and obstacles that can obstruct an individual's path.

> One must conquer the mind. It is through the mind that one experiences both bondage and liberation. (6:6)

Here, Lord Krishna emphasizes the importance of conquering the mind. The mind can be a source of turmoil and distraction, leading to inner conflicts and battles. By gaining control over one's thoughts and emotions, an individual can find inner peace and liberation from the struggles of the mind.

> Yield not to unmanliness, O son of Pritha! It does not suit you. Cast off this base faint-heartedness and arise, O

> scorcher of enemies!" (2:3)

Lord Krishna encourages Arjuna to rise above fear and weakness, urging him to fulfill his duty as a warrior. This verse highlights the need to confront challenges with courage and determination. It signifies that one must face the battles of life head-on, rather than succumbing to despair or resignation.

> One who performs their duty without attachment, surrendering the results unto the divine, is unaffected by sinful action, as the lotus leaf is untouched by water. (5:10)

In this verse, Lord Krishna advises the importance of performing one's duty without attachment to the outcomes. Life's battles often involve making difficult choices and acting, but the focus should be on performing one's responsibilities selflessly, without being overly concerned about success or failure. Just as a lotus leaf remains untouched by water, a person who acts without attachment remains unaffected by the negative consequences of their actions.

> You have the right to perform your prescribed duty, but you are not entitled to the fruits of your actions. Never consider yourself the cause of the results of your activities, and never be attached to not doing your duty.(2:47)

Lord Krishna advises Arjuna that one should focus on performing their duties without attachment to the outcomes. By relinquishing the desire for personal gain and surrendering the fruits of actions to a higher power, individuals can maintain equanimity and freedom from the burden of success or failure.

> On this path, effort never goes to waste, and there is no

> failure. Even a little practice of this discipline protects one from great fear. (2:40)

Lord Krishna assures Arjuna that any effort made on the path of righteousness and self-realization is never in vain. Even a small step towards spiritual growth and self-improvement yields significant benefits and protects one from immense suffering and fear.

> One who has control over the mind is tranquil in heat and cold, in pleasure and pain, and in honor and dishonor; and is ever steadfast with the Supreme Self. (6:7)

Here is the Lord highlights the importance of developing mental equanimity and control. By mastering the mind and detaching oneself from external circumstances, one can remain steady and undisturbed amidst life's fluctuations and challenges. The battle lies in attaining inner stability and aligning oneself with the higher Self.

> The soul is neither born, and nor does it ever die; nor having once existed, does it ever cease to be. The soul is unborn, eternal, ever-existing, undying and primeval. (2:20)

Lord Krishna explains the eternal nature of the soul. Life's battles and challenges are temporary, while the essence of our being, the soul, is eternal and indestructible. Recognizing this truth can provide solace and perspective, reminding us that our struggles are transitory in the larger context of our immortal souls.

These verses from the Bhagavad Gita offer deeper insights into the concept of life as a battlefield, emphasizing the need for self-discipline, detachment, and spiritual awareness in navigating the challenges and adversities of existence.

The Gita provides guidance on virtues to cultivate and pitfalls to avoid in the battle of life. Here are some virtues recommended by the Gita, along with corresponding verses:

1. Detachment: The Gita emphasizes the importance of performing one's duties without attachment to the outcomes. Detachment helps maintain equanimity and freedom from the bondage of desire.

   > You have the right to perform your prescribed duty, but you are not entitled to the fruits of your actions. Never consider yourself the cause of the results of your activities, and never be attached to not doing your duty. (2:47)

2. Selflessness: Acting selflessly and dedicating one's actions to a higher purpose, rather than seeking personal gain, is considered virtuous.

   > Therefore, without being attached to the fruits of activities, one should act as a matter of duty, for by working without attachment, one attains the Supreme. (3:19)

3. Equanimity: Cultivating mental balance and maintaining composure in the face of challenges and ups and downs of life is crucial. It involves accepting both pleasure and pain with equanimity.

   > He who can withstand the impulses of lust and anger before the attainment of salvation, is self-disciplined and happy within, and is the true yogi and divine being. (5:23)

4. Wisdom: Seeking knowledge, self-realization, and a deeper understanding of the true nature of the self and the universe is highly valued in the Gita.

   That knowledge by which one undivided spiritual nature is seen in all living entities, though they are divided into innumerable forms, you should understand to be in the mode of goodness. (18:20)

Additionally, the Gita warns against certain pitfalls to avoid in the battle of life:

1. Attachment to desires and outcomes: Excessive attachment to the results of actions can lead to suffering and dissatisfaction. The Gita advises performing actions without being overly attached to the fruits.

    > Perform your duties, but without attachment, for the man who performs his duties without attachment attains the Supreme. (3:19)

2. Ego and pride: The Gita highlights the destructive nature of ego and pride, which can cloud judgment and lead to arrogance.

    > Pride, arrogance, conceit, anger, harshness, and ignorance—these qualities belong to those of demonic nature, O son of Pritha. (16:18)

By cultivating virtues like detachment, selflessness, equanimity, and wisdom, while avoiding the pitfalls of attachment, ego, and pride, one can navigate the battle of life with greater clarity, inner strength, and spiritual growth.

Battle for God's Sake Alone

In life's great battle, virtues lead the way,
In Krishna's words, their truths we shall convey.
Let's delve into the virtues we must embrace,
And shed the attributes that bring us disgrace.

Detachment first, the key to inner peace,
From outcomes freed, our strivings find release.
Perform our duties, yet let go of gain,
For selfless acts are virtues we attain.

With equanimity, we face life's tide,
Both pleasure's waves and pain's fierce tempests ride.
A steady mind, unmoved by worldly sway,
In battles fought, our calmness lights the way.

Selflessness, a beacon bright and pure,
Transcending self, compassion we ensure.
Dedicating actions to a higher cause,
Our souls expand, finding our source.

Wisdom sought, the light of knowledge's grace,
Unveiling truth, illuminating space.
In self-realization, we find the key,
To conquer ignorance and truly be free.

Now, let us shun the attributes unwise,
That clouds our vision and veil truth's sunrise.
Attachment's chains, release them, let them go,
And taste the freedom that detachment bestows.

Ego, that fickle foe, we must subdue,
For in its grip, our virtues we undo.
Humility and grace, our virtues soar,
Ego's fall reveals the depths of our core.

And as we march, these virtues held in heart,
The fruits of victory, they shall impart.
Inner peace, a treasure deep and divine,
A life well-lived, a victory that shines.

In battles fought, with virtues as our guide,
The battle won, our spirits unified.
With wisdom, selflessness, and calm we thrive,
And taste the victory in every stride.

This battlefield of life, where struggles abound,
The Lord's words shall resound.
Let virtues shine, and darkness subside,
As we explore the battle's ebb and tide.

Courage, the stalwart virtue we embrace,
Amidst adversity, it finds its place.
With valiant hearts, we face each daunting foe,
In battles fought, our inner strength will grow.

Compassion blooms, a virtue pure and bright,
In helping others, we find our own light.
With empathy, we heal wounds deep and wide,
To forge connections that shall never divide.

Wisdom, the guiding star within our souls,
Illuminates paths where knowledge unfolds.
Through seeking truth, our minds shall find release,
Enlightenment's embrace, our hearts find peace.

Temperance, a virtue to gently hold,
In passions' flames, it keeps us from growing cold.
With balanced hearts, we navigate life's storm,
And find serenity in its graceful form.

Yet, as we tread this battlefield of strife,
Certain attributes we must avoid in life.
Arrogance, a vice that blinds us to truth,
With humility, we restore our youth.

Greed, a sly temptress, must be cast aside,
Contentment found in treasures that reside,
Not in possessions, but in souls we meet,
Love's richness shared, a victory complete.

With virtue as our armor, firm and strong,
We battle vices that have done us wrong.
And in the triumph of our virtuous fight,
The fruits of victory shine so bright.

Inner peace, the reward we seek to gain,
When harmony within our hearts shall reign.
A life well-lived, a legacy we leave,
In virtues nurtured, with love we weave.

Let us go forth, with virtues as our guide,
In this grand battle, side by side.
With love, compassion, courage, and much more,
We rise above the battlefield's uproar.

The Goal of Life

Various goals of life and paths to attain them are discussed in the Gita – here are some of them along with verses that illustrate them:

1. Immortality (Amrita):

    For the soul there is neither birth nor death at any time. He has not come into being, does not come into being, and will not come into being. He is unborn, eternal, ever existing, and primeval. He is not slain when the body is slain. (2:20)

2. Unity with Brahman (Brahma-Nirvana):

    That which is night for all beings is the time of awakening for the self-controlled; and the time of awakening for all beings is night for the introspective sage. (2:72)

3. Unity with Ishvara (Yoga):

    For one who sees Me everywhere and sees everything in Me, I am never lost, nor is he ever lost to Me. (6:30)

4. Freedom from suffering (Moksha):

    One who is not disturbed in mind even amidst the threefold miseries or elated when there is happiness, and who is free from attachment, fear, and

> anger, is called a sage of steady mind. (2:56)

5. Self-realization (Atma-Jnana):

> A person is said to have achieved yoga, the union with the Self, when the perfectly disciplined mind gets freedom from all desires and becomes absorbed in the Self alone. (6:8)

6. Performing duties without attachment (Nishkama Karma):

> You have the right to perform your prescribed duty, but you are not entitled to the fruits of your actions. Never consider yourself to be the cause of the results of your activities, and never be attached to not doing your duty. (2:47)

7. Devotion to God (Bhakti):

> To those who are constantly devoted to serving Me with love, I give the understanding by which they can come to Me. (9:22)

The Gita explores various aspects of life, spirituality, and the pursuit of ultimate truth, providing guidance on how to live a righteous and fulfilling life while attaining liberation from the cycle of birth and death. There are also a variety of people who have different goals as well as those with different in-born talents and tendencies.

Lord Krishna also mentions intermediate stages of attainment since some seekers are content to stay in way stations while others continue to reach some final destination:

1. Attaining divine qualities (Daivi Sampad):

   > Fearlessness, purity of heart, steadfastness in knowledge and yoga, charity, control of the senses, performance of sacrifice, study of scriptures, austerity, straightforwardness, nonviolence, truthfulness, absence of anger, renunciation, tranquility, aversion to fault-finding, compassion for all living entities, freedom from covetousness, gentleness, modesty, and steady determination, vigor, forgiveness, fortitude, cleanliness, freedom from malice, and absence of haughtiness—these, O scion of the Bharata dynasty, are born of divine qualities. (16:1-3)

2. Selfless service (Nishkama Seva):

   > Therefore, without being attached to the fruits of activities, one should act as a matter of duty, for by working without attachment, one attains the Supreme. (3:19)

3. Spiritual knowledge (Jnana):

   > I shall now explain the knowable, knowing which you will taste the eternal. Brahman, the spirit, beginningless and subordinate to Me, lies beyond the cause and effect of this material world. (13:11)

4. Cultivating inner peace (Shanti):

   > One who is not disturbed in mind even amidst the threefold miseries or elated when there is happi-

> ness, and who is free from attachment, fear, and anger, is called a sage of steady mind. (2:66)

5. Achieving divine union (Bhagavat-Sannidhi):

> And yet, those who fix their minds on Me and engage in devotional service with steadfast determination, I consider them to be the most perfect. (12:7)

While the Lord discusses various goals of life, there is a common theme that runs through them all. The central theme of the Gita is the attainment of spiritual realization and liberation (Moksha) through the path of self-realization, devotion, and righteous action.

Though the Gita mentions multiple goals, they are not contradictory but interconnected. The different goals represent various paths or approaches to spiritual growth, and they are often complementary rather than contradictory.

The underlying message of the Gita is to encourage individuals to live a life of righteousness, duty, and selflessness while recognizing the eternal nature of the soul and the interconnectedness of all beings. It emphasizes the importance of self-discipline, selfless action, devotion to God, and the cultivation of spiritual knowledge and virtues.

Ultimately, the Gita teaches that all these goals converge toward the realization of one's true nature, which is unity with the Supreme, be it through self-realization, devotion, or righteous action. The common thread is the pursuit of spiritual growth and the realization of the eternal truth.

It's important to approach the Gita holistically, understanding that the various goals and paths are meant to cater to different individuals with their unique inclinations, temperaments, and stages of spiritual evolution. The diversity of goals and paths in the Gita reflects the richness and inclusiveness of the Divine Krishna, accommodating different approaches towards spiritual progress while emphasizing the ultimate goal of self-realization and liberation.

Make Your Life Meaningful

In life's vast journey, myriad goals arise,
With paths diverse, where seekers turn their eyes.
Immortal quest, to transcend finite breath,
And taste eternity, escape from death.

Some seek union with Brahman, boundless truth,
In cosmic oneness, find eternal youth.
Through selfless acts, they strive to be set free,
From samsara's cycle, and worldly decree.

In devotion's embrace, hearts find their way,
To Ishvara, divine, where spirits sway.
With love profound, their souls in surrender,
Merge with the divine, in blissful splendor.

Freedom from suffering, the goal pursued,
Through wisdom's light, ignorance subdued.
Renouncing attachments, tranquil minds grow,
Peace dawns within, as sorrows cease to flow.

Each seeker treads a path, unique and rare,
To self-realization, answers to bear.
Nishkama Karma, deeds with no desire,
Serve humanity, selfless acts inspire.

In soul's progression, divine qualities bloom,
Fearlessness, compassion, banish all gloom.
With knowledge's flame, ignorance does wane,
To reveal truths deep, unbound by the mundane.

The theme entwined in these diverse pursuits,
The unity of souls, where truth transmutes.
In righteous action, love, and pure intent,
Lies liberation's call, all souls are meant.

So, in life's tapestry, diverse threads weave,
A grand symphony, where souls seek to cleave.
Embrace the goals, the journey's ceaseless stride,
To find the truth, in unity abide.

The spiritual teacher

The Gita doesn't provide an extensive commentary on the role of a spiritual teacher or guru; however, it does offer some insights. We should also understand that in essence, the Guru is one with the Divine Personality of God. Let's explore these teachings in detail:

1. Importance of seeking guidance:

   The Gita emphasizes the significance of seeking guidance from a realized spiritual teacher. In Chapter 4, Verse 34, Lord Krishna advises Arjuna:

   Just try to learn the truth by approaching a spiritual master. Inquire from him submissively and render service unto him. The self-realized souls can impart knowledge unto you because they have seen the truth.

This verse emphasizes the need to approach a spiritual teacher with humility, surrender, and a genuine desire to learn.

2. The role of the guru:

   The Gita acknowledges the vital role of a spiritual teacher in guiding individuals on the path of self-realization. In Chapter 4, Verse 42, Lord Krishna explains:

   Know that all states of being—be they of goodness, passion, or ignorance—are manifested by My energy. I am, in one sense, everything, but I am independent. I am not under the modes of material nature, for they, on the contrary, are within Me.

The guru is an embodiment of divine consciousness and is not bound by the limitations of material existence. The guru's teachings and guidance help individuals realize their own divine nature.

3. Transmitting spiritual knowledge:

   The Gita emphasizes the transmission of spiritual knowledge from the guru to the disciple. In Chapter 13, Verse 2, Lord Krishna describes the qualities of a true guru:

   This body, O son of Kunti, is called the field, and one who knows this body is called the knower of the field by those who truly understand."

Here, the guru is portrayed as one who possesses true knowledge and can impart the understanding of the self and the material body to the seeker.

4. Surrendering to the guru:

   The Gita emphasizes the significance of surrendering to a spiritual teacher and following their guidance wholeheartedly. In Chapter 18, Verse 66, Lord Krishna advises Arjuna:

   Abandon all varieties of religion and just surrender unto Me. I shall deliver you from all sinful reactions. Do not fear.

While this verse specifically refers to surrendering to Lord Krishna, it can also be interpreted as surrendering to a genuine spiritual teacher who leads the disciple toward liberation. Surrendering to the guru involves placing complete trust in their guidance and relinquishing ego-driven desires and attachments.

5. Personal experience and realization:

   The Gita emphasizes the importance of personal experience and realization in spiritual growth. In Chapter 9, Verse 2, Lord Krishna explains:

   This knowledge is the king of education, the most secret of all secrets. It is the purest knowledge and because it gives direct perception of the self by realization, it is the perfection of religion. It is everlasting, and it is joyfully performed.

Here, the Gita suggests that the teachings of a spiritual teacher should lead to direct personal realization and inner experience of the truths being taught. The guru guides the seeker in acquiring knowledge that brings about self-realization and leads to the highest spiritual attainment.

The verses referenced above highlight the significance of approaching a guru with humility, the role of the guru as a transmitter of spiritual knowledge, the need for surrender and trust, and the ultimate goal of personal realization.

The Gita also provides insights into the qualifications of the guru, and the role they play in guiding the spiritual student. Here are some key qualifications of a guru and what they can do for the spiritual student:

1. Self-realization and knowledge:

A qualified guru possesses self-realization and deep spiritual knowledge. In Chapter 4, Verse 34, Lord Krishna counsels:

Just try to learn the truth by approaching a spiritual master. Inquire from him submissively and render service unto him. The self-realized souls can impart knowledge unto you because they have seen the truth."

This verse emphasizes that a genuine guru is one who has realized the truth and can impart that knowledge to the student.

2. Exemplary conduct:

A qualified guru leads a life of integrity and practices what they teach. In Chapter 3, Verse 21, Lord Krishna advises Arjuna:

Whatever action a great person performs, common people follow. And whatever standards they set by exemplary acts; all the world pursues."

This verse suggests that a guru's conduct sets an example for others to follow, inspiring students to walk the path of righteousness.

3. Compassion and guidance:

A qualified guru possesses compassion and provides guidance to the spiritual student. In Chapter 10, Verse 11, Lord Krishna reveals His divine manifestations to Arjuna:

To show them special mercy, I, dwelling in their hearts, destroy the darkness born of ignorance with the shining lamp of knowledge."

Here, Lord Krishna explains that the guru, as an embodiment of divine knowledge, dispels the ignorance of the student through compassionate guidance and illuminates their path with spiritual wisdom.

4. Liberation and spiritual growth:

   A qualified guru helps the spiritual student attain liberation and facilitates their spiritual growth. In Chapter 18, Verse 66, Lord Krishna advises Arjuna:

   Abandon all varieties of religion and just surrender unto Me. I shall deliver you from all sinful reactions. Do not fear."

In this verse, while specifically referring to surrendering to Lord Krishna, it implies that surrendering to a genuine guru who leads the student toward liberation can free them from the bondage of ignorance and worldly attachments.

5. Personal transformation and realization:

   A qualified guru facilitates the personal transformation and realization of the spiritual student. In Chapter 9, Verse 22, Lord Krishna describes the process of transformation through devotion:

   To those who are constantly devoted and who engage in worship with a pure mind, I carry what they lack and preserve what they have.

This verse indicates that a qualified guru helps the student in their spiritual journey by supporting their progress, providing what is needed, and safeguarding their spiritual well-being.

In summary, the qualifications of a guru include self-realization, deep spiritual knowledge, exemplary conduct, compassion, and the ability to guide students toward liberation. A genuine guru facilitates the spiritual growth and transformation of the student, helping them attain self-realization, providing guidance and support, and ensuring their overall well-being on the spiritual path.

The teachings of the Bhagavad Gita emphasize the significance of finding a qualified guru who can impart spiritual knowledge, lead by example, and guide the student toward enlightenment and liberation.

Guru is God, God is Guru

In still mind wisdom's light forever gleams,
A guide emerges, seeker's heart it deems.
With self-realization's touch profound,
A guru's grace in silence can be found.

His knowledge flows, a sacred stream of truth,
Unveiling mysteries, eternal youth.
In conduct pure, His life's example shines,
Inspiring hearts, igniting sacred lines.

Compassion guides, with gentle words to steer,
Dispelling darkness, bringing vision clear.
Through guidance wise, they lead every soul's ascent,
To liberation's shore, all karma spent.

Transformation blooms, soul set free,
Union deep, divine love's symphony.
The guru's gift, a journey's sacred thread,
A bridge to realms where ego's chains are shed.

Seek the guide, whose light shines bright within,

His presence - the key to self, now begin,

With trust and surrender, paths intertwine,

In union deep, seeking soul now align.

In sacred bond, a dance of heart and mind,

A guru's touch, a treasure rare to find.

Through grace bestowed, the seeker finds release,

A glimpse of truth, an everlasting peace.

Three Yoga Paths Are One

Traditionally, there are supposed to be three main types of yoga discussed in the Gita: Karma Yoga, Bhakti Yoga, and Jnana Yoga. Each type of yoga is associated with a different path to spiritual realization and is described in various verses throughout the Gita. Here's an explanation of each type along with multiple verses for each:

1. Karma Yoga (Yoga of Action):

   Karma Yoga is the path of selfless action, where individuals perform their duties without attachment to the outcomes or personal desires. It emphasizes the idea of offering one's actions to a higher power, seeking spiritual growth through selflessness and service to others.

   Verses highlighting Karma Yoga:

   a) You have the right to perform your prescribed duty, but you are not entitled to the fruits of your actions. Never consider yourself the cause of the results of your activities, and never be attached to not doing your duty. (2:47)

   b) Without being attached to the fruits of activities, one should act as a matter of duty, for by working without attachment, one attains the Supreme. (3:19)

   c) One who performs his duty without attachment, surrendering the results unto the Supreme Lord, is unaffected by sinful action, as the lotus leaf is untouched by water. (5:10)

2. Bhakti Yoga (Yoga of Devotion):

   Bhakti Yoga is the path of devotion and love towards a personal deity or a divine power. It involves cultivating a deep emotional connection and surrendering to the divine through prayer, worship, and meditation. Bhakti Yoga emphasizes the notion of selfless love and union with the divine.

   Verses highlighting Bhakti Yoga:

   a) Even those who are devoted to other deities with faith, they too, O son of Kunti, worship Me alone, though following the wrong method. (9:23)

   b) And I am the basis of the impersonal Brahman, which is immortal, imperishable, and eternal and is the constitutional position of ultimate happiness. (14:27)

   c) And of all yogis, the one with great faith who always abides in Me, thinks of Me within himself, and renders transcendental loving service to Me – he is the most intimately united with Me in yoga and is the highest of all. That is My opinion. (6:47)

3. Jnana Yoga (Yoga of Knowledge):

   Jnana Yoga is the path of knowledge and wisdom. It involves deep contemplation, self-inquiry, and the discernment of the true nature of reality. Jnana Yoga aims at realizing the ultimate truth and attaining liberation through the cultivation of spiritual knowledge.

   Verses highlighting Jnana Yoga:

a) For one who has taken his birth, death is certain; and for one who is dead, birth is certain. Therefore, in the unavoidable discharge of your duty, you should not lament. (2:27)

b) The soul is neither born, and nor does it die at any time. It does not come into being again when the body is created. The soul is birthless, eternal, imperishable, and timeless and is never terminated when the body is terminated. (2:20)

c) That which pervades the entire body, know it to be indestructible. No one is able to destroy the imperishable soul." (2:17)

These three paths of yoga, Karma Yoga, Bhakti Yoga, and Jnana Yoga are not mutually exclusive but rather complement each other. They represent different approaches to spiritual growth and self-realization, catering to the diverse nature of individuals and their preferences.

It is important to note that the Gita does not promote one type of yoga as superior to others. Instead, it encourages individuals to choose the path that resonates with them and practice it wholeheartedly. The Gita teaches that all paths lead to the ultimate truth and realization of the divine.

By engaging in selfless actions (Karma Yoga), cultivating devotion and love (Bhakti Yoga), and seeking spiritual knowledge (Jnana Yoga), individuals can progress on their spiritual journey and attain liberation (moksha) from the cycle of birth and death.

It is worth mentioning that the Gita also describes other forms of yoga such as Dhyana Yoga (meditation), Dhyana Yoga (Yoga of Meditation), and Sankhya Yoga (Yoga of Knowledge and Analysis). These additional paths further enrich the spiritual teachings of the Gita.

Most commentators teach that by practicing any of these paths sincerely, individuals can progress spiritually and realize their true nature. However, it may also be the intent of Lord Krishna that for some practitioners, an integrated path comprising of all three major yogas form a coherent whole and can lead to a greater realizations.

Indeed, the three aspects of Kriya Yoga as defined by Patanjali—Tapas (discipline), Svadhyaya (self-study), and Ishvara Pranidhana (surrender to the divine)—can be correlated with the three main types of yoga mentioned in the Bhagavad Gita. Here's an explanation of how these aspects align, along with relevant verses from the Gita and the Yoga Sutras:

1. Tapas (Discipline) - Correlated with Karma Yoga:

   Tapas refers to the practice of discipline and self-control, which is essential for spiritual growth. Similarly, Karma Yoga emphasizes performing one's duties selflessly, without attachment to the outcomes.

   Verse from the Gita:

   One who restrains the senses and organs of action but whose mind dwells on sense objects certainly deludes oneself and is called a pretender. (Gita 3:6)

Verse from the Yoga Sutras (Patanjali):

Discipline, austerity, self-study, and surrender to the Supreme Being constitute Kriya Yoga. (Yoga Sutras 2.1)

2. Svadhyaya (Self-Study) - Correlated with Jnana Yoga:

   Svadhyaya refers to the practice of self-study and self-reflection, leading to the cultivation of spiritual knowledge. Jnana Yoga also emphasizes the pursuit of knowledge and discernment of the true nature of reality.

   Verse from the Gita:

   Whenever and wherever, there is a decline in religious practice, O descendant of Bharata, and a predominant rise of irreligion—at that time I descend Myself." (Gita 4:7)

   Verse from the Yoga Sutras (Patanjali):

   "Study of sacred texts, repetition of sacred sounds, and reflection on divine principles constitute Svadhyaya." (Yoga Sutras 2.1)

3. Ishvara Pranidhana (Surrender to the Divine) - Correlated with Bhakti Yoga:

   Ishvara Pranidhana refers to surrendering oneself to the divine, acknowledging a higher power and seeking union through devotion. Bhakti Yoga emphasizes devotion and love for a personal deity or divine power.

   Verse from the Gita:

   And of all yogis, the one with great faith who always abides

> in Me, thinks of Me within himself, and renders transcendental loving service to Me – he is the most intimately united with Me in yoga and is the highest of all. That is My opinion. (Gita 6:47)
>
> Verse from the Yoga Sutras (Patanjali):
>
> To achieve surrender to the Supreme Being and attain samadhi (union) is Ishvara Pranidhana. (Yoga Sutras 2.1)

These correlations between the aspects of Kriya Yoga and the three types of yoga described in the Gita (refer figure 3) demonstrate their interconnectedness and compatibility. They provide a comprehensive framework for individuals to progress on their spiritual journey by cultivating discipline, self-study, and surrender to the divine.

GITA	YOGA SUTRAS	MOKSHA
KARMA YOGA Ch. 1-6	Tapas	Self-Realization
BHAKTI YOGA Ch. 7-12	Ishwar Pranidhan	God Realization
GYANA YOGA Ch. 13-18	Swadhaya	Cosmic Consciousness

Figure 3: Gita and Kriya Yoga

Integrated Three-fold Path to Liberation

In paths of ancient wisdom, three unfold,
Their essence captured in verses told.
Kriya Yoga's aspects, pure and serene,
Hamsas in the skies, let their beauty be seen.

First, Tapas' fire, discipline so true,
A flame that burns, igniting virtues anew.
With steadfast resolve, actions selfless, pure,
Karma Yoga's grace, its essence secure.

Svadhyaya, self-study, next in line,
Delve deep within a radiant shrine.
In rhythmic strokes, explore wisdom's sea,
Jnana Yoga's call, to know and to be free.
Embrace Ishvara Pranidhana, surrender's plea,
Bhakti Yoga's devotion, hearts set free.
With love profound, the divine we embrace,

In sacred space, find solace and grace.

Tapas, Svadhyaya, and Ishvara's call,
KriyaYoga's trifecta, weaving a thrall.
In soul's triumph, that truth we find,
United in harmony, body, soul, and mind.

Let Krishna's words guide our sacred quest,
In rhythmic breath, our spirits blessed.
KriyaYoga's essence, in median flow,
With each gentle heartbeat, our union shall grow.

These paths converge, in harmonious blend,
Gunas three, in unity transcend.
Wisdom light unfold, in beat of Om,
KriyaYoga's science, a transformative art

Jivatma

The Gita explores the concepts of Atma, Jivatma, and Paramatma in the context of the eternal soul and its relationship with the Supreme Being. These concepts are deeply intertwined and are elucidated throughout the Gita. Here are a few verses that shed light on their meaning and relationship:

1. Atma:

   The term "Atma" refers to the individual soul or self. It is the eternal essence that resides within every living being, transcending the physical body and mind. The Gita describes Atma as indestructible, immutable, and divine in nature.

   For the soul atma, there is neither birth nor death at any time. It has not come into being, does not come into being, and will not come into being. It is unborn, eternal, ever existing, and primeval. He is not slain when the body is slain. (2:20)

2. Jivatma:

   Jivatma is the individual soul or consciousness that is embodied within a living being. It represents the subjective experience of an individual and is often considered a reflection of the supreme consciousness. The Gita emphasizes the idea of self-realization and the importance of recognizing the Jivatma as distinct from the physical body and mind.

> Just as a person puts on new garments after discarding the old ones, similarly, the soul Jiva acquires new bodies after casting away the old and useless ones. (2:22)

3. Paramatma:

   Paramatma refers to the Supreme Soul or the Divine Self, which transcends individuality and encompasses the entire universe. It is the ultimate reality from which all beings arise and with which they ultimately merge. The Gita teaches that realizing the unity of one's individual soul (Jivatma) with the Supreme Soul (Paramatma) leads to spiritual liberation.

   > He is the source of all lights, beyond darkness, the knowledge and the object of knowledge, seated in the hearts of all beings. (13:17)

   > I am the Self, O Gudakesha, seated in the hearts of all creatures. I am the beginning, the middle, and the end of all beings. (10:20)

These verses highlight the interconnectedness and hierarchical relationship between Atma, Jivatma, and Paramatma. The Jivatma, or individual soul, is an eternal entity that can realize its true nature by recognizing its unity with the Paramatma, the Supreme Soul. Through self-realization and devotion, one can attain liberation and merge with the divine essence.

In Advaita, Brahman is the ultimate reality, the supreme cosmic power, and the source of all existence. Brahman is often considered synonymous with Paramatma, the Supreme Soul, while Atma and Jivatma are understood to be individual manifestations or reflections of Brahman. Here are a few verses from the Bhagavad Gita that illuminate the relationship between Brahman and the concepts of Atma, Jivatma, and Paramatma:

1. Brahman as the ultimate reality:

   Brahman is described as the eternal, unchanging, and all-pervading reality that underlies and sustains the entire universe.

   I am the basis of the imperishable and the eternal, the unmanifested and of eternal virtue. (14:27)

2. Atma and Jivatma as manifestations of Brahman:

   Atma and Jivatma, representing the individual souls, are considered as distinct but inseparable from Brahman. They are seen as expressions or individual reflections of the supreme reality.

   The living entities in this conditioned world are My eternal fragmental parts. Due to conditioned life, they are struggling very hard with the six senses, which include the mind. (15:7)

3. Realizing the identity of Jivatma and Paramatma with Brahman:

   The Gita teaches that by realizing the true nature of the individual soul (Jivatma) as being inseparable from the Supreme Soul (Paramatma), one can recognize their identity with Brahman and attain spiritual liberation.

   One who is thus transcendentally situated at once realizes

the Supreme Brahman and becomes fully joyful. He never laments nor desires to have anything; he is equally disposed to every living entity. In that state, he attains pure devotional service unto Me. (18:55)

4. Unity with Brahman through devotion and surrender:

   The Gita emphasizes the path of devotion and surrender as a means to realize the unity with Brahman. By offering one's actions, thoughts, and self to the Supreme, one can merge with Brahman and attain liberation.

   To those who are constantly devoted and who engage in the devotional service with love, I give the understanding by which they can come to Me. (9:22)

These verses illustrate the relationship between Brahman, Atma, Jivatma, and Paramatma. Brahman is the ultimate reality, while Atma and Jivatma are individual manifestations or reflections of Brahman. Recognizing the identity of Jivatma with Paramatma, and ultimately with Brahman, is considered the path to spiritual liberation and union with the supreme cosmic power.

In the Gita, Lord Krishna is the manifestation of Ishvara, the Supreme Being or God, who possesses infinite power, knowledge, and compassion. The relationship between Ishvara and the concepts of Atma, Jivatma, Paramatma, and Brahman can be understood as follows:

1. Ishvara as the controller and source of all:

   Ishvara is described as the creator, sustainer, and destroyer of the universe. All beings, including Atma, Jivatma, Paramatma, and Brahman, are ultimately under the control and guidance of Ishvara.

I am the source of all spiritual and material worlds. Everything emanates from Me. The wise who know this perfectly engage in My devotional service and worship Me with all their hearts. (10:8)

2. Jivatma and Paramatma as manifestations of Ishvara:

   Jivatma, the individual soul, and Paramatma, the Supreme Soul, are considered manifestations of Ishvara. While Jivatma represents the individual consciousness, Paramatma represents the divine presence within all beings.

   I am the Self, O Gudakesha, seated in the hearts of all creatures. I am the beginning, the middle, and the end of all beings. (10:20)

3. Ishvara's relationship with Atma and Jivatma:

   Ishvara is intimately connected with Atma and Jivatma, as the ultimate controller and the source of their existence. Ishvara guides and supports the individual souls, offering them opportunities for growth and spiritual realization.

   The Supreme Lord is situated in everyone's heart, O Arjuna, and is directing the wanderings of all living entities, who are seated as on a machine, made of the material energy. (18:61)

4. Realizing the identity of Jivatma with Ishvara:

   The Gita emphasizes that recognizing the identity of Jivat-

> ma with Ishvara is a crucial step in spiritual evolution. By understanding that the individual soul is an eternal part of the Supreme Soul, one can establish a profound connection with Ishvara.
>
> Always think of Me, become My devotee, worship Me, and offer your homage unto Me. Thus, you will come to Me without fail. I promise you this because you are My very dear friend. (18:65)

These verses illustrate the relationship between Ishvara, Atma, Jivatma, Paramatma, and Brahman. Ishvara is the Supreme Being, the controller and source of all existence. Atma and Jivatma are considered as manifestations of Ishvara, and Paramatma represents the divine presence within all beings. Realizing the identity of Jivatma with Ishvara is emphasized as a means to establish a deep connection with the Supreme and attain spiritual fulfillment.

Soulfoulness

Within the ancient script of Gita's lore,
Reside the truths of souls and realms divine.
Atma, Jivatma, Paramatma, explore
Concepts entwined, their mystic ties align.

Atma, the soul, eternal and profound,
Transcends the mortal coil, unbound by strife.
Intrinsic essence, pure and ever-crowned,
Immortal spark, the tapestry of life.

Jivatma, soul individualized,
Reflects the cosmic essence, intertwined.
Within each being, it's realized,
The microcosm, with macrocosm aligned.

Paramatma, the Supreme Soul divine,
Transcendent, all-pervading cosmic force.
To every heart, its presence does enshrine,
The source from which all life's currents course.

Now Brahman, the ultimate reality,
The cosmic tapestry's eternal thread.
In Brahman's embrace, souls find unity,
The oneness where creation's truths are spread.

Ishvara, God, the ruler and the guide,
Creator, sustainer, boundless in grace.
In hearts, where Jivatma does reside,
Ishvara's love illuminates each space.

Heart of heart, wisdom's truths unfold,
Revealing the connections, strong and clear.
Through souls and God, their interweaving told,
The cosmic dance of life, sublime yet near.

The Gunas

According to the Gita, the three Gunas are the three fundamental qualities or attributes that pervade all of creation. These Gunas are called Sattva (goodness), Rajas (passion), and Tamas (ignorance). Here are some verses from the Gita that elaborate on these Gunas and their effects on humanity:

1. **Sattva (Goodness):**

   Knowledge, action, and the doer—these are declared in the scriptures to be of three kinds, according to the Gunas, as also are the objects of knowledge, action, and the doer. (Gita 18.19)

Sattva represents purity, knowledge, harmony, and spiritual enlightenment. It is characterized by peace, clarity, and a sense of balance. When the Sattva Guna predominates, individuals tend to possess virtues such as compassion, wisdom, and selflessness. Sattva promotes spiritual growth and leads to liberation.

More verses that explain Sattva and its effects:

1. Sattva, being pure, is illuminating and free from disease. It binds by attachment to happiness and knowledge. (Gita 14.6)

Sattva is characterized by the qualities of purity, clarity, and illumination. It brings about a sense of well-being, contentment, and joy. It also leads to the pursuit of knowledge and spiritual growth. However, Sattva can also bind individuals through attachment to happiness and knowledge, as excessive attachment can hinder spiritual progress.

2. The mode of goodness conditions one to happiness; knowledge, peace, and wisdom are its by-products." (Gita 14.6)

Sattva creates a conducive environment for experiencing joy, peace, and contentment. Sattva also fosters the development of knowledge, wisdom, and a deep sense of inner peace. When Sattva predominates, individuals are inclined towards virtuous actions and exhibit qualities such as compassion, selflessness, and harmony.

3. The mode of goodness, O Arjuna, prevails by suppressing Rajas and Tamas. It manifests as knowledge, and it attaches one to happiness. Negating sorrow, it binds one to happiness." (Gita 14.11)

Sattva prevails by subduing the influence of Rajas and Tamas. It manifests as knowledge, leading to the expansion of consciousness and understanding. Sattva creates an attachment to happiness and negates sorrow, binding individuals to joy and contentment. It helps individuals overcome negative tendencies and promotes overall well-being.

The Gita encourages individuals to cultivate Sattva and maintain a balanced state of mind where Sattva predominates over Rajas and Tamas. By embracing the qualities of Sattva, individuals can experience greater clarity, inner peace, and spiritual growth. Sattva facilitates the path towards self-realization and liberation from the limitations imposed by the other Gunas.

2. Rajas (Passion):

> Know that as attachment, desire, and craving are the causes of all misery, so do I declare, O Arjuna, that anger is the root cause of ignorance. It is born of Rajas, and it is insatiable and greatly sinful." (Gita 14.12)

Rajas represents activity, ambition, restlessness, and passion. It is associated with the ego, desires, and the pursuit of worldly goals. When Rajas dominates, individuals tend to be driven by desires, seeking personal gain and success. However, excessive Rajas can lead to attachment, dissatisfaction, and suffering.

Here are more verses about Rajas and its effects:

1. Know that Rajas, which is born of desire and attachment, is the cause of all actions. O Arjuna, understand Rajas to be of the nature of passion, which binds the embodied soul with attachment to the fruits of action. (Gita 14.7)

Rajas is born from desires and attachments - it is the driving force behind actions and motivates individuals to pursue their goals. However, Rajas also binds the soul to attachment, making one focused on the outcomes and results of their actions rather than the actions themselves. This attachment can lead to restlessness and dissatisfaction.

2. The mode of passion is characterized by incessant craving and attachment, and it binds the embodied soul through attachment to the fruits of work. O Arjuna, this mode is insatiable and gives rise to endless desires. (Gita 14.12)

Rajas is also characterized by incessant craving and attachment

- leading to a constant desire for more and binds individuals through attachment to the results of their actions. This attachment fuels an insatiable nature, where desires seem endless, and satisfaction becomes elusive. Rajas can lead to restlessness, impatience, and an intense focus on material achievements.

3. Attachment, desire, and hankering after success—these arise from Rajas. O Arjuna, know that this is the root of all troubles and suffering. (Gita 14.12)

While Rajas provides the impetus for action, excessive attachment and desires can lead to various troubles and suffering. When individuals are driven solely by the pursuit of worldly achievements, they may neglect their spiritual well-being and experience inner turmoil.

The Gita encourages individuals to strive for a balanced state where the influence of Rajas is moderated by Sattva, the Guna of goodness and harmony. By cultivating Sattva, one can channel their passion and energy in a positive and balanced manner, leading to personal growth, fulfillment, and spiritual progress.

3. Tamas (Ignorance):

> Now hear from Me, O Arjuna, about the threefold division of faith, in accordance with the Gunas—Sattva, Rajas, and Tamas." (Gita 17.2)

Tamas represents inertia, darkness, ignorance, and delusion. It is associated with laziness, ignorance, and a lack of awareness. When Tamas prevails, individuals become lethargic, deluded, and prone to negative tendencies. They may be driven by ignorance, laziness, and indulge in harmful activities, leading to stagnation and suffering.

The Gunas are not static; they interact and influence one another. Each person possesses a unique combination of these Gunas, and their proportions may change over time based on their actions, environment, and state of mind. The goal of spiritual growth, according to the Gita, is to transcend the limitations of the Gunas and attain a state of pure consciousness beyond their influence.

Tamas, the Guna of ignorance and inertia, is described in the Bhagavad Gita through various verses. Here are a couple of them that shed light on Tamas and its effects:

1. When there is an increase in Tamas and a decrease in Sattva and Rajas, O Arjuna, know that to be the influence of Tamas. (Gita 14.13)

This verse explains that when Tamas becomes predominant and outweighs the qualities of Sattva and Rajas, it influences an individual's thoughts, actions, and mindset. Tamas brings about a state of darkness and inertia, which can lead to ignorance, confusion, and a lack of motivation or initiative.

2. The mode of darkness, born of ignorance, deludes all embodied beings. It binds the consciousness, stupefying them with laziness, sleep, and heedlessness. (Gita 14.8)

Tamas clouds the understanding and perception of reality, leading to delusion. It binds the consciousness, making one unaware of their true potential and the path of spiritual growth. Laziness, sleepiness, and carelessness become prevalent, hindering personal development and progress.

3. The outcome of Tamas is delusion, ignorance, and negligence. O Arjuna, those who are of a deluded nature, never achieve self-realization nor do they reach success or happiness. (Gita 14.12)

Being dominated by Tamas leads to delusion, where one loses sight of their true nature and the path of self-realization. Ignorance prevails, preventing individuals from understanding deeper truths and hindering spiritual growth. As a result, success and true happiness remain elusive.

The Gita does not condemn any of the Gunas but encourages individuals to transcend them. Tamas, in its balanced and controlled form, has its role in rest and rejuvenation. However, excessive Tamas can hinder personal growth and spiritual progress. The goal is to cultivate Sattva, the Guna of goodness and clarity, which helps overcome the limitations of Tamas and Rajas, leading to higher states of consciousness and self-realization.

Here are a few reasons why the Gita emphasizes the need to overcome the Gunas:

1. Liberation from suffering: The Gunas, especially Rajas and Tamas, bind individuals to the cycle of desires, attachments, and ignorance, which can lead to suffering and dissatisfaction. Overcoming the Gunas allows one to rise above these limitations and experience liberation from the cycle of birth and death.

2. Self-realization: The ultimate goal of human life, according to the Gita, is to realize one's true nature as the eternal soul (Atman) beyond the transient physical and men-

tal states. The Gunas, particularly Tamas and Rajas, cloud our understanding and hinder us from realizing our true selves. By transcending the Gunas, we can attain self-realization and experience our divine essence.

3. Spiritual growth and evolution: The Gunas are part of the cosmic order and play a role in shaping our experiences and actions. However, being overly influenced by Rajas and Tamas can hinder spiritual growth. By cultivating Sattva and transcending the lower Gunas, we can align ourselves with higher principles and values, leading to personal evolution and spiritual progress.

4. Attainment of higher states of consciousness: The Gunas are associated with different levels of consciousness. Tamas represents a lower state of consciousness, Rajas represents a restless and ego-driven state, while Sattva represents a higher state of consciousness characterized by purity, wisdom, and inner peace. Overcoming the Gunas allows one to ascend to higher levels of consciousness and experience a deeper connection with the divine.

By cultivating Sattva and aligning their actions with spiritual principles, one can attain a state of equanimity, peace, and harmony, and ultimately realize their true nature as an eternal spiritual being beyond the realm of the Gunas.

The Gita provides guidance on how to overcome the Gunas and rise above their influence. Here are a few verses that illustrate the process of transcending the Gunas:

1. By practicing discrimination, one can transcend the in-

fluence of the three Gunas that arise from the material nature and achieve liberation from birth, death, old age, and disease. (Gita 14.20)

This verse highlights the importance of discrimination (Viveka) in transcending the Gunas. Discrimination refers to the ability to discern between the eternal and the temporary, the real and the unreal. By cultivating discrimination, individuals can rise above the influence of the Gunas and attain liberation from the cycle of life and death.

2. When one rises above the three Gunas that arise from the body, one is freed from birth, death, old age, and all kinds of distress, and one attains spiritual realization." (Gita 14.21)

The Gita emphasizes that rising above the Gunas leads to freedom from suffering and spiritual realization. By transcending the limitations imposed by the Gunas, individuals can experience a state of liberation, where they are no longer subject to the fluctuations of the material world and its accompanying distress.

3. When one fully understands the nature of Sattva, Rajas, and Tamas and transcends them, one becomes established in pure transcendental knowledge. (Gita 14.20)

This verse suggests that by cultivating awareness and understanding of the Gunas, one can transcend them. When individuals develop a deep insight into the nature and effects of Sattva, Rajas, and Tamas, they can gradually rise beyond their influence. This understanding leads to the realization of pure transcendental knowledge, which is beyond the Gunas.

4. Mentally renouncing all actions, constantly centered in the self, with body and mind controlled, free from possessiveness and ego, one attains tranquility. (Gita 18.49)

This verse teaches the path to transcending the Gunas through self-control, renunciation, and a shift in perspective. By letting go of attachment, ego, and possessiveness, and by cultivating a state of mental detachment from the fruits of actions, individuals can attain tranquility and rise above the Gunas.

The process of overcoming the Gunas involves self-awareness, discrimination, self-control, and a dedicated spiritual practice. By cultivating qualities such as purity, wisdom, and selflessness, individuals can gradually transcend the limitations of the Gunas and attain higher states of consciousness, leading to spiritual growth and liberation.

Letting Go of the Gunas

In rhythmic lines, with grace and subtle flow,
Krishna's wisdom reveals the path to sow.
The Gunas three, their hold on us so tight,
In verses grand, their essence takes its flight.

To transcend these Gunas and reach the light,
Discrimination's flame must burn bright.
By knowing the eternal from transient strife,
We rise above, attaining truest life.

Through understanding, we break free and soar,
Above the cycles that bind us evermore.
Birth, death, old age, and suffering's sting,
No longer can they claim us as their king.

With focused mind, renouncing actions' claim,
Centered in self, we find peace's sweet refrain.
Let not possessiveness or ego's sway,
Impede our journey towards eternal day.

In tranquil states, the Gunas lose their might,
As self-control and wisdom guide us right.
Detached from fruits, we forge a higher way,
Beyond the Gunas' grip, we gently sway.

In every verse, the Gita's wisdom gleams,
Revealing how to transcend these earthly streams.
With grace and purpose, we strive to be,
Above the Gunas, soaring, ever free.

So let us heed the Gita's sacred voice,
Embrace its teachings, make the conscious choice.
To rise above the Gunas' binding chain,
And in pure transcendence, eternal bliss attain.

In verses sung with poetic finesse,
The Gita's wisdom imparts ways to address.
The Gunas' hold, their sway on mortal hearts,
Through eloquent lines, their essence imparts.

To overcome these Gunas, seek the light,
With discrimination, shining clear and bright.
Distinguish the eternal from the transient haze,
Transcending limitations in wisdom's blaze.

By grasping knowledge, their clutches we break,
Liberated from cycles that cause us to ache.
No more shall birth, death, or aging constrain,
When Gunas' dominance we dare to disdain.

In self-awareness, the path is unveiled,
Renouncing actions, the ego's grip curtailed.
Centered within, finding tranquil repose,
In the sanctuary of self, true freedom flows.

Let go of possessiveness and desires,
For they hinder progress, quench the soul's fires.
With self-control, in mastery we stand,
Free from the grasp of the Gunas' demand.

Detach from the fruits of actions we sow,
Unburdened, towards enlightenment we go.
In tranquil states, Gunas lose their hold,
As wisdom guides, our spirits unfold.

Through every verse, the Gita's teachings ring,
Guiding us to transcendence on wisdom's wing.
Embrace its words, let them light your way,
Beyond the Gunas, to realms of eternal day.

With grace and purpose, journey forth, my friend,
In pursuit of liberation, let your spirit ascend.
The Gita's verses, a beacon for your soul,
Leading you beyond Gunas' earthly control.

So heed its call, let its wisdom be your guide,
In every step, let your inner light decide.
Transcending the Gunas, reaching heights untold,
Union with the divine, your true self to unfold.

Renunciation, Selfless Action and Duty

Renunciation, also known as sannyasa or the path of renunciation, is a concept deeply rooted in various spiritual and religious traditions. It involves letting go of attachments to worldly possessions, desires, and ego in order to attain spiritual liberation or enlightenment. Renunciation is often associated with a life of simplicity, detachment, and selflessness, where one's focus shifts from external pursuits to inner growth and realization of the ultimate truth.

In the Sanatana Dharma, renunciation is one of the four ashramas (stages of life) prescribed in the ancient texts known as the Vedas. The fourth stage, called sannyasa, is meant for individuals who have fulfilled their responsibilities as householders and are ready to dedicate themselves fully to spiritual pursuits. The Gita discusses the importance and significance of renunciation in several verses. One such verse is:

Renunciation is declared to be of three kinds, O Arjuna, according to the three modes of material nature. The acts of sacrifice, charity, and penance are not to be given up; they must be performed. Indeed, sacrifice, charity, and penance purify even the great souls. (18.4)

Lord Krishna emphasizes that renunciation does not mean abandoning all actions or responsibilities but rather performing them with the right understanding and attitude. It highlights those acts of sacrifice, charity, and penance, when performed without attachment or selfish motives, can purify and uplift the individual.

In Buddhism, renunciation is an essential aspect of the Noble Eightfold Path, which is the path to end suffering and attain enlightenment. The Buddha taught that attachment and craving are the root causes of suffering, and by renouncing desires and attachments, one can break free from the cycle of suffering. The Dhammapada, a collection of the Buddha's teachings, contains verses that convey the importance of renunciation. One such verse states:

Let go of the past,

Let go of the future,

Let go of the present,

And cross over to the farther shore of existence.

With mind wholly liberated,

You shall come no more to birth and death. (Dhammapada 348)

The Lord Buddha emphasizes the need to let go of attachments to the past, future, and present, as they bind individuals to the cycle of birth and death. By renouncing these attachments and freeing the mind from all grasping, one can attain liberation from the suffering of existence.

In the teachings of Advaita Vedanta, a non-dualistic philosophy within Hinduism, renunciation is seen as a means to transcend the illusory world and realize one's true nature as the ultimate reality (Brahman). It involves renouncing the identification with the body, mind, and ego, and recognizing oneself as the eternal, unchanging consciousness. The following verse from the ancient text Yoga Vasistha highlights this concept:

Renunciation is of two kinds: that which is practiced by those who withdraw from worldly life, and that which is practiced mentally by those who are still engaged in worldly life. The former is the renunciation of external objects, while the latter is the renunciation of the mind's attachment to those objects. (Yoga Vasistha 3.7.4)

Rishi Vasistha explains that renunciation can be practiced externally by withdrawing from worldly pursuits, as well as internally by cultivating detachment and non-attachment while still being engaged in worldly activities. Both forms of renunciation ultimately lead to the realization of one's true nature.

Overall, the concept of renunciation encompasses letting go of attachments, desires, and ego in order to attain spiritual liberation, enlightenment, or self-realization. It is a central theme in various spiritual traditions, emphasizing the importance of living a spiritual life in a material world.

The concept of renunciation can appear to contradict the emphasis on action - the Gita resolves this apparent contradiction by teaching the principle of selfless action, known as Nishkama Karma Yoga. It encourages individuals to perform their duties and responsibilities without attachment to the results or personal desires. Let's explore some verses from the Gita that shed light on this resolution:

1. You have the right to perform your prescribed duty, but you are not entitled to the fruits of your actions. Never consider yourself the cause of the results of your activi-

ties, and never be attached to not doing your duty. (2.47)

This verse teaches that individuals have the right to engage in actions but should not be motivated by personal desires or become attached to the results. By practicing selfless action, one can maintain equanimity and detachment.

2. Perform your duty equipoised, O Arjuna, abandoning all attachment to success or failure. Such equanimity is called yoga. (2.48)

Here, Lord Krishna advises Arjuna to carry out his duty with equanimity, irrespective of success or failure. This verse emphasizes the need to cultivate a balanced and detached mindset while engaging in action. By renouncing attachment to the outcomes, one can attain a state of inner harmony and spiritual union (yoga).

3. He who performs his duty without attachment, surrendering the results unto the Supreme Lord, is unaffected by sinful action, as the lotus leaf is untouched by water. (5.10)

It is important to surrender the fruits of one's actions to the Supreme. By offering the results of one's efforts to a higher power and performing actions without attachment, one transcends the karmic consequences and remains unaffected by the material world.

4. One who performs his duty without attachment, who is devoted to the Supreme Lord, who is a pure soul, and who has conquered his mind and senses is neither affected by sinful action nor entangled while performing his prescribed duties. (18.17)

This verse describes someone who performs their duties without attachment, with devotion to the Supreme, and with control over their mind and senses. Such a person remains unaffected by the consequences of their actions and is not bound by the entanglements of material existence.

The Gita resolves the apparent contradiction between renunciation and action by advocating for selfless action. By renouncing the ego's desires and offering the results of actions to the Supreme, one can achieve inner harmony, spiritual growth, and liberation from the cycle of karma.

The Gita teaches that renunciation and selfless action can be practiced by individuals while engaging in the world and help them achieve liberation. Here are some verses that highlight this aspect:

1. Without being attached to the fruits of activities, one should act as a matter of duty, for by working without attachment, one attains the Supreme. (3.19)

By acting selflessly, fulfilling their responsibilities as a matter of duty, and not seeking personal gain, individuals can attain a higher state of consciousness and come closer to realizing the Supreme.

2. A person in the divine consciousness, although engaged in seeing, hearing, touching, smelling, eating, moving about, sleeping, and breathing, always knows within himself that he actually does nothing at all. (5.8)

One can engage in worldly activities while maintaining a state of inner awareness and detachment. Those who are established in divine consciousness understand that their true Self, the eternal soul, remains unaffected by external actions and experiences.

3. One who performs his prescribed duty without any self-centered motives, without attachment to the results, and without being influenced by the modes of material nature is said to be truly renounced. (18.9)

When actions are performed with a sense of duty, without being influenced by material desires or the fluctuations of the mind, one can attain the state of true renunciation.

4. The yogis, abandoning attachment, act with body, mind, intelligence, and even with the senses, only for the purpose of purification. (5.11)

Yogis act in the world with their body, mind, intelligence, and senses, but without attachment. Their actions are solely aimed at purifying themselves and attaining spiritual growth.

By performing one's duties without attachment to the outcomes, acting with a sense of duty and without self-centered motives, individuals can cultivate a state of inner detachment, awareness, and spiritual progress. Through this practice, they can experience the harmony of renunciation and selfless action in their everyday lives.

In the Gita there isa significant emphasis on the role of duty in the practice of renunciation and selfless action. Duty, known as "swadharma," refers to the responsibilities and obligations that are inherent to an individual based on their inherent nature, social position, and stage of life. Here are some verses that highlight the relationship between duty, renunciation, and selfless action:

1. Better is one's own duty, though imperfectly performed, than the duty of another well executed. It is better to die in one's own duty; the duty of another is fraught with fear. (3.35)

This verse stresses the importance of adhering to one's own duty, even if it is not performed perfectly, rather than engaging in the duty of another. It implies that each individual has a unique set of responsibilities and obligations in life, and renunciation involves embracing and fulfilling those duties selflessly.

2. It is far better to discharge one's prescribed duties, even though they may be faulty, than another's duties perfectly. Destruction in the course of performing one's own duty is better than engaging in another's duties, for to follow another's path is dangerous. (3.41)

Like the previous verse, this one emphasizes that fulfilling one's own duties, even with imperfections, is superior to performing someone else's duties flawlessly. It emphasizes the importance of staying true to one's own responsibilities and not being swayed by the allure of others' paths.

3. Considering your specific duty as a kshatriya, you should know that there is no better engagement for you than fighting on religious principles; and so there is no need for hesitation." (2.31)

In the above verse, Lord Krishna advises Arjuna, who was a warrior (kshatriya) by birth, to recognize his duty and embrace it fearlessly. This verse suggests that fulfilling one's duties in accordance with one's inherent nature and social position is essential, even if it involves challenges or difficult choices.

4. One's own duty, even if without excellence, is preferable to another's duty well-performed. Dying while performing one's duty is better; others' duties are fraught with fear." (18.47)

Lord Krishna once again reiterates the idea that performing one's own duty, even with imperfections, is more valuable than engaging in another person's duty. It emphasizes that it is better to live and die while fulfilling one's own responsibilities than to take up the responsibilities of others out of fear or desire.

These verses collectively emphasize the significance of recognizing and embracing one's own duty. Renunciation and selfless action are not about abandoning responsibilities but rather performing them with a sense of duty and selflessness, without attachment to the outcomes. By fulfilling one's inherent responsibilities and obligations, individuals can progress spiritually, maintain inner harmony, and contribute to the greater welfare of society.

Renunciation in Action

On spiritual path, we explore with care,
Renunciation's role, its purpose fair.
Concept of letting go, attachments shed,
To find enlightenment where ego's dead.

Sanatana Dharma speak of stages in life,
Sannyasa, fourth ashrama in their strife.
Performing duty without desire's sway,
The Lord's lay guides us on this way.

He teaches selfless action's crucial part,
Detach from outcomes, duty in the heart.
True renunciation, duties fulfilled,
Transcend material world, in spirit stilled.

Guatama too, renunciation finds space,
Craving and attachment it seeks to erase.
Dhammapada's verses, wisdom profound,
Letting go, liberation can be found.

Advaita Vedanta, non-duality's path,
Renounce identification, ego's wrath.
Rishi Vasistha shares his timeless view,
Internal renunciation, truth in you.

So, renunciation's essence we discern,
Performing duties, lessons we should learn.
Selfless action and letting go we find,
Inner peace and liberation aligned.

Duty plays a pivotal role, we see,
In renunciation and selfless decree.
Sanatana Dharma, scriptures wise and old,
Speak of duty's importance, truth now told.

Fulfilling responsibilities we bear,
Embracing swadharma with utmost care.
Each person has a unique role to play,
In society's fabric, come what may.

The Gita urges us to perform our task,
With selflessness, a noble and virtuous ask.
Imperfectly done, yet true to our own,
Duty's fulfillment, seeds of growth are sown.

One's duty, though flawed, is preferred choice,
Than another's duty performed with poise.
Staying true to our path, not swayed astray,
Duty's call, the righteous, fearless way.

Through duty, we progress and spiritually rise,
Maintain harmony, a life that satisfies.
Contribution to society's greater good,
Duty's fulfillment, a noble livelihood.

So, duty intertwines with renunciation's art,
Performing selfless actions, playing our part.
In fulfilling duties, we display our ray,
Renunciation and duty, a unified way.

Dispassion and Renunciation

Dispassion, or detachment, is the state of being free from excessive attachment to worldly desires and outcomes. Here are a few verses from the Gita that elucidate its teachings on dispassion:

1. Chapter 2, Verse 56:

    Those who are unaffected by external influences, remaining equipoised in pleasure and pain, established in knowledge, they attain immortality.

When one remains unaffected by external circumstances and maintains equanimity, true dispassion arises, and one is not swayed by the dualities of pleasure and pain but instead remains established in knowledge.

2. Chapter 2, Verse 58:

    One who can withdraw the senses from their objects just as a tortoise withdraws its limbs within the shell, such a person is established in divine wisdom.

When the practitioner withdraws the senses from their objects - symbolizing the need to control desires and avoid becoming excessively attached - this withdrawal leads to the establishment of divine wisdom, which is only possible through dispassion.

3. Chapter 3, Verse 34:

    Senses are said to be superior (to the gross body); the mind is superior to the senses; the intellect is superior to the mind; that which is superior to the intellect is the Self.

There is a hierarchy of consciousness. By recognizing the supremacy of the Self beyond the intellect, one can develop dispassion towards the incessant demands and fluctuations of the mind, senses, and body.

4. Chapter 5, Verse 7:

   Renouncing the fruit of action, the disciplined self attains the state of eternal peace; whereas the one who, out of desire, acts with attachment, being bound by those actions, remains in bondage.

By performing actions without attachment to their outcomes and renouncing the desire for the fruits of one's actions, an individual can attain eternal peace. Acting with dispassion frees one from the cycle of attachment and bondage.

5. Chapter 18, Verse 16:

   When knowledge is covered by ignorance, and wisdom is concealed by that which is contrary to wisdom, that deluded understanding, enveloped in darkness, leads to an understanding opposed to truth.

Attachment arises from the delusions caused by ignorance. When knowledge is overshadowed by ignorance and desire, one's understanding becomes clouded. Dispassion allows for clarity of understanding, enabling the realization of truth.

The process of maintaining equanimity, withdrawing from sensory desires, recognizing the supremacy of the Self, renouncing attachment to outcomes, and avoiding the delusions of ignorance and desire is practicing dispassion. Through this process, one can cultivate inner peace, spiritual growth, and a deeper understanding of oneself and the world.

Dispassion and renunciation are closely interconnected and work together to guide individuals on the path of spiritual growth and liberation. In the Gita, the state and process of yoga is almost synonymous with dispassion:

1. Chapter 6, Verse 2:

   What is called renunciation, know that to be yoga. One cannot become a yogi without renouncing the desire for fruits of actions.

True renunciation is not merely the external act of giving up worldly possessions or responsibilities. Renunciation, in its essence, is the relinquishment of attachment to the outcomes of our actions. By renouncing the desire for the fruits of our actions, we cultivate dispassion and detach ourselves from the fluctuations of the material world.

2. Chapter 18, Verse 2:

   The giving up of the fruits of all activities is called renunciation by the wise. And that state is said to be yoga, the state of perfect peace."

Renunciation is described as the act of surrendering the results of our actions. By letting go of the attachment to the outcomes, we cultivate a state of peace and harmony. This renunciation leads us towards dispassion, enabling us to act selflessly and with equanimity.

3. Chapter 18, Verse 52:

    When your intellect crosses the mire of delusion, you will then acquire a state of indifference to what has been heard and what is yet to be heard.

Worldly delusions are transcended through the power of discernment. When we develop dispassion, we cultivate an attitude of indifference towards external opinions and the constant desire for new information. We become steadfast in our knowledge and establish ourselves in a state of inner tranquility.

4. Chapter 18, Verse 66:

    Abandon all varieties of religion and just surrender unto Me. I shall deliver you from all sinful reactions. Do not fear.

It is not easy to develop dispassion by merely thinking about it and Lord Krishna gives the way of surrendering to the divine - this surrender requires renunciation of all forms of religious dogma and attachment to external rituals. Through this surrender, dispassion naturally arises as we let go of our egoic desires and trust in a higher power.

Dispassion and mind control are interconnected aspects of spiritual practice in the Gita. The teachings emphasize the importance of disciplining the mind and cultivating dispassion to attain inner peace and spiritual growth. Let's explore some verses that shed light on the relationship between dispassion and mind control:

1. Chapter 6, Verse 25:

    Gradually, through regular practice and detachment, the

> mind becomes controlled, and attains a state of tranquility.

This verse highlights the role of detachment, which is closely related to dispassion, in controlling the mind. By practicing detachment from worldly desires and outcomes, the mind gradually becomes disciplined and attains a state of tranquility.

2. Chapter 6, Verse 26:

> From wherever the restless and unsteady mind wanders, one must bring it back under the control of the Self alone.

The spiritual student needs to bring the wandering and restless mind under control. Dispassion plays a vital role in this process, as it enables us to detach ourselves from the distractions that pull the mind outward. By redirecting the mind towards the Self, we can achieve greater control over its fluctuations.

3. Chapter 18, Verse 33:

> Knowledge, the object of knowledge, and the knower – these three, when they function together, are in a mode of goodness. The absence of attachment, the absence of aversion, and balanced mind – these three, when they function together, are considered to be in the mode of passion.

This verse highlights the importance of cultivating a balanced mind through dispassion. When the mind is free from attachment and aversion, it becomes balanced and steady. Dispassion allows us to transcend the extremes of craving and aversion, leading to a more controlled and balanced state of mind.

By cultivating dispassion, we develop the ability to detach ourselves from the constant fluctuations of desires and attachments. This detachment supports the process of mind control, allowing us to discipline the restless mind and attain a state of tranquility. In turn, a controlled mind further strengthens our practice of dispassion, creating a harmonious cycle of growth and spiritual progress.

Dispassion

In paravasta, where wisdom supreme dwell,
A path unfolds, where seekers bid farewell,
To transient joys that bind the mortal heart,
And in dispassion's light, find their true part.

Renunciation, key to freedom's gate,
Is not in casting off life's earthly weight,
But in releasing clutch of desire's hold,
To seek within, where treasures manifold.

With disciplined mind, a tranquil sea,
The torrents of thoughts find serenity,
For in the stillness, liberation gleams,
Where ego's sway dissolves in sacred streams.

The restless mind, a challenge to command,
Yet dispassion's touch brings strength to withstand,
Attachments' grip, desires' seductive lure,
In noble quest, the ego's reign ensure.

Through dispassion's lens, perceptions refined,
A balanced soul transcends the ties that bind,
And as the mind finds mastery's embrace,
Liberation dawns, unveiling grace.

In this dance divine, where hearts ascend,
Dispassion, renunciation blend,
Mind's control, a gateway to the sublime,
In liberation's realm, state beyond time.

Liberation, Self-realization and Wisdom

Terms like wisdom, self-realization and liberation are carelessly bandied about without true understanding. While they share common goals and principles, they offer slightly different perspectives on the ultimate spiritual attainment. It is helpful for the spiritual student to consider what the Gita has to say about these states:

1. Liberation (Moksha):

   Those who are free from false prestige, illusion, and false association, who understand the eternal, who are done with material lust, who are freed from the dualities of happiness and distress, and who, without delusion, know how to surrender unto the Supreme Person, attain to that eternal kingdom. (15.5)

Lord Krishna speaks of liberation or moksha, which refers to the liberation from the cycle of birth and death, and attaining union with the eternal divine. It involves transcending the material world and realizing one's true nature as an eternal spiritual being. Liberation is the goal, where one achieves freedom from suffering and attains eternal bliss.

2. Self-Realization (Atma-jnana):

   When a sensible man ceases to see different identities due to different material bodies and he sees how beings are expanded everywhere, he attains to the Brahman conception. (13.31)

Lord Krishna highlights the concept of Self-Realization or Atma-jnana, which is the realization of one's own true self or Atman. It involves understanding the eternal, indivisible nature of the Self beyond the limitations of the physical body and the identification with the material world. Self-Realization leads to a deep understanding of one's true essence as an eternal, conscious being.

While liberation and Self-Realization are distinct in their focus, they are interconnected. Self-Realization is a crucial step on the path to liberation. By realizing one's true Self and transcending identification with the temporary aspects of existence, an individual can attain liberation from the cycle of birth and death.

Self-Realization is a significant step towards attaining liberation, as it enables individuals to understand their eternal nature and transcend the limitations of the material world. Both concepts of Liberation and Self-Realization are essential in the spiritual journey towards ultimate liberation and union with the divine.

Wisdom plays a crucial role in the path of liberation and Self-Realization. The Gita emphasizes the connection between wisdom, liberation, and Self Realization through various verses. Here are a few verses that illustrate this connection:

1. When a person dwells in his mind on the object of sense gratification, attachment to them is born. From attachment, desire arises, and from desire, anger arises. (2.62)

Attachment and desires bind us to the cycle of birth and death, hindering our spiritual progress. By recognizing the transient nature of worldly pleasures, we can cultivate detachment and move closer to liberation.

2. One who can withdraw his senses from sense objects, as the tortoise draws its limbs within the shell, is firmly fixed in perfect consciousness. (2.58)

By disciplining our senses and turning our attention inward, we develop a state of heightened awareness and clarity. This detachment from external distractions allows us to connect with our true nature and move towards Self Realization.

3. One who performs his duty without attachment, surrendering the results unto the Supreme Lord, is unaffected by sinful action, as the lotus leaf is untouched by water. (5.10)

By dedicating our actions to a higher purpose and surrendering the results to a higher power, we free ourselves from the burdens of success or failure. This selfless attitude fosters spiritual growth and liberation from the cycle of karma.

4. He alone sees truly who sees the Lord present equally in all creatures, the Imperishable amidst the perishable. (13.27)

By realizing the unity and interconnectedness of all life, we develop a sense of compassion and oneness. Through this vision of the divine in everything, we transcend limited identifications and move closer to Self-Realization.

5. One who sees inaction in action and action in inaction is intelligent among men, and he is in the transcendental

position, although engaged in all sorts of activities. (4.18)

True action transcends mere physical activity. It implies that while engaging in the world, one can maintain a state of inner stillness and detachment. Through this understanding, we can perform our duties with a sense of equanimity, unaffected by the external outcomes.

By developing wisdom through cultivating detachment, self-discipline, selfless action, recognizing the divine in all, and maintaining equanimity, individuals can progress on the path towards liberation and attain Self Realization:

1. The wise, by means of meditation on the Self, realize the eternal, indivisible, omnipresent, and immutable Reality. They attain liberation from the cycle of birth and death and become free from all sorrows. (2.72)

The wisdom, gained through deep contemplation and meditation on the true Self, leads to the realization of the eternal and unchanging Reality. By understanding our essential nature as eternal beings beyond the temporary physical existence, we attain liberation from the cycle of birth and death and transcend all sorrows.

2. The man who sees me in everything and everything within me will not be lost to me, nor will I ever be lost to him. (6.30)

Here, Lord Krishna emphasizes the wisdom of perceiving the divine presence in all beings and recognizing the inherent unity in creation. By developing this all-encompassing vision, one moves closer to Self-Realization and liberation, as they understand the interconnectedness of all life and their inherent oneness with the divine.

3. That knowledge by which one sees the undivided, unmanifested, indivisible Supreme Being dwelling in all beings, is knowledge in the mode of goodness. It liberates one from all material bondage. (Gita 18.20)

The knowledge that enables one to perceive the supreme presence pervading all beings and the universe is considered knowledge in the mode of goodness. This knowledge leads to liberation by freeing one from material bondage, helping them realize their true nature.

4. When your intelligence has passed out of the dense forest of delusion, you shall become indifferent to all that has been heard and all that is to be heard. (2.52)

Wisdom enables one to transcend the delusions and illusions of the material world. When one's intelligence is awakened and freed from ignorance, they become indifferent to the distractions and superficialities of the world, focusing instead on the pursuit of Self-Realization and liberation.

Wisdom is intricately connected to liberation and Self-Realization. Through deep contemplation, meditation, and the cultivation of spiritual knowledge, one gains the wisdom to see beyond the illusions of the material world and realize their true nature. This wisdom leads to liberation from the cycle of birth and death and facilitates the attainment of Self- Realization, where individuals recognize their inherent divinity and the unity of all existence.

Self Peace

Realms of wisdom's boundless, sacred grace,
Where truths of liberation find their rightful place,
Time unfolds, weaving a sacred rhyme divine,
On Self-Realization, eternal and sublime.

Piercing the veil, wisdom's light shall brightly shine,
Revealing paths that lead to the divine.
From ancient scriptures' depths, we glean,
Timeless truths of liberation's eternal sheen.

Liberation, freedom from worldly chains that bind,
Release from suffering's grasp, the seeking mind.
Transcend the cycle of birth and death's cruel strife,
Merge with the eternal, embracing everlasting life.

Wisdom's gentle whispers guide with tender care,
As we seek truths hidden in the ethereal air.

In meditation's embrace, our minds find rest,
Self-Realization awakened within our chest.

To know the Self, beyond illusion's guise,
In stillness and silence, where truth lies.
The divine essence, unchanging, ever near,
In every form, its presence crystal clear.

Wisdom teaches us to see with eyes anew,
Beyond the surface, where eternal truths accrue.
The unity of all, in every form and hue,
From dewdrop's grace to the sky's infinite blue.

With every breath, let our souls aspire,
To quench the longing, reach higher and higher.
Through Self-Realization, merge, and unite,
With the timeless Self, bathed in eternal light.

Oh, wisdom's beacon, guide us on our way,
Illuminate our path, each and every day.

Liberation's bliss, may it embrace us tight,
As we journey within, on wings of endless flight.

In the realm of mind, let these concepts bloom,
An ode to liberation, dispelling all gloom.
Through the dance of self with Self, hearts ignite,
With the fire of wisdom, burning ever bright.

Compassion versus Duty

In the Gita, there are several verses that highlight the interconnection between compassion and selflessness:

1. Chapter 12, Verse 13:

   He who hates no creatures, and is friendly and compassionate to all, who is free from possessiveness and egoism, balanced in pleasure and pain, and forgiving, that devotee is dear to me.

Lord Krishna encourages us to let go of hatred, possessiveness, and ego, and instead cultivate forgiveness and a balanced approach to life.

2. Chapter 16, Verse 3:

   The divine qualities lead to liberation, whereas the demoniac qualities bind one to the cycle of birth and death. O son of Pandu, do not worry, for you are born with divine qualities.

The divine qualities referred to are compassion, selflessness, and love that lead to liberation and spiritual growth. By embodying these qualities, one transcends the cycle of birth and death and experiences higher states of consciousness.

3. Chapter 18, Verse 41:

   Those who are possessed by egoism and power, who are hypocritical and arrogant, who perform actions

> out of pride and personal desire, they are deluded by ignorance and act against their own self-interest.

Th Gita warns against the dangers of egoism, arrogance, and selfish actions. It encourages individuals to act with humility, selflessness, and compassion, recognizing that such actions align with their true nature and lead to inner harmony.

In the Gita, there is a challenging situation where the duty of a warrior, like Arjuna, conflicts with the principles of compassion and non-violence and Lord Krishan has to address this apparent contradiction:

1. Chapter 2, Verse 31:

   Considering your dharma (duty) as a warrior, you should not waver. Indeed, there is nothing better for a warrior than a righteous war.

First of all, Lord Krishna encourages Arjuna to recognize his duty as a warrior and emphasizes that engaging in a righteous war is in line with his dharma. While compassion is important, there are circumstances where fulfilling one's duty takes precedence.

2. Chapter 2, Verse 33:

   If, however, you do not fight this battle of dharma, then, by giving up your personal and social duties, you will certainly incur sin.

By avoiding his duty, Arjuna would be neglecting his personal and social responsibilities. Failing to fulfill one's obligations can lead to negative consequences and a sense of guilt or sin.

3. Chapter 2, Verse 47:

> You have a right to perform your prescribed duty, but you are not entitled to the fruits of your actions. Never consider yourself the cause of the results of your activities, and never be attached to not doing your duty.

The solution is that individuals have the right to perform their prescribed duties but should not be attached to the outcomes. It emphasizes the importance of acting selflessly and without ego, understanding that the consequences are not entirely within our control.

4. Chapter 18, Verse 17:

> That which in the beginning may appear as poison, but at the end is like nectar, and which awakens one to self-realization, that understanding is said to be in the mode of goodness.

Lord Krishna points out that sometimes actions that seem harsh or unpleasant initially may ultimately lead to a greater good or realization. The duty to fight in a righteous war, even against one's kin, may serve a higher purpose such as upholding justice and preserving righteousness.

The Gita acknowledges the apparent contradiction between compassion and the duty to fight but provide guidance on understanding the context, recognizing one's duty, and acting without attachment. They remind us that sometimes fulfilling our obligations, even in difficult circumstances, can lead to positive outcomes and inner growth.

Compassion is the virtue of feeling deep empathy and kindness towards all beings. It involves treating others with love, understanding, and respect, regardless of their circumstances or actions. The Gita emphasizes the importance of cultivating compassion as a means of fostering harmony and spiritual growth.

Selflessness refers to the act of putting others' needs and well-being before one's own. It involves transcending selfish desires and ego and acting for the benefit of others. Selflessness is seen as a path to liberation, as it frees one from the cycle of attachment and allows for a broader perspective beyond personal interests.

Duty, or dharma, is the inherent responsibility and role that each individual has in life. It encompasses both personal and social obligations. The Gita teaches that fulfilling one's duty is crucial, as it contributes to the overall welfare of society and maintains cosmic order. Duty is seen as a means to express one's true nature and contribute to the greater good.

These concepts are intertwined - individuals should act with compassion and selflessness while also fulfilling their prescribed duties. It encourages individuals to recognize the interconnectedness of all beings and to navigate ethical dilemmas by balancing compassion with the fulfillment of responsibilities, using selflessness as the foundation.

Compassion

In hearts we find compassion's gentle call,
To see beyond ourselves, embrace all.
Selfless acts, with ego's chains unbound,
In service to others, love's depths profound.

Duty, beacon light guiding our true way,
A path of righteousness, come what may.
When enemies arise, both out and in,
We face them boldly, battles try to win.

With courage firm, we fight against the tide,
No challenge too great, no foe can hide,.
In unity, we rise, a valiant band,
To vanquish darkness, on noble ground we stand.

Through conflict's storms, compassion shall prevail,
For even in war, love's light won't fail.
In victory or loss, we'll heed the call,
To kill the enemy, yet rise above all.

Yoga in Devotion and Devotion in Yoga

The Gita provides insights into various aspects of spiritual life, including the path of devotion (Bhakti Yoga). Devotion in the Gita refers to the unwavering love and surrender of an individual towards the divine, and it emphasizes the significance of developing a personal relationship with God. Here are some key verses from the Gita that elucidate its teachings on devotion:

1. Fix your mind on Me, be devoted to Me, offer service to Me, bow down to Me, and you shall certainly reach Me. I promise you because you are very dear to Me. (18.65)

Lord Krishna emphasizes the importance of fixing one's mind on Him and developing a deep devotion. He assures that those who are devoted to Him with love and surrender will undoubtedly attain Him.

2. Those who worship Me with devotion, meditating on My transcendental form, to them I carry what they lack and preserve what they have. (9.22)

He assures that those who worship Him with genuine devotion and contemplate His divine form will be taken care of by Him. He states that He will provide whatever is lacking and protect whatever is already possessed by the devotees.

3. Engage your mind always in thinking of Me, become My devotee, offer obeisance to Me and worship Me. Being

completely absorbed in Me, surely you will come to Me. (9.34)

This highlights the significance of continuously contemplating and remembering the divine. Lord Krishna encourages individuals to engage their minds in thoughts of Him, be devoted to Him, and offer reverence and worship. By being completely absorbed in God, one can ultimately reach Him.

4. The one who loves Me alone with undivided love, worships Me in all beings, resides in Me, whatever be his mode of life, that yogi lives in Me. (6.30)

Lord Krishna emphasizes the all-encompassing nature of devotion. He states that a true devotee is one who loves God with undivided love and sees the divine presence in all living beings. Such a devotee, irrespective of their way of life, remains connected to God and resides in Him.

5. Even those who are devoted to other deities with faith, they also worship Me alone, O son of Kunti, but in an improper way. (9.23)

Lord Krishna explains that those who worship other deities with faith are indirectly worshipping Him. However, He points out that their devotion is not proper because they lack a complete understanding of His supreme nature. He encourages them to direct their devotion towards the ultimate divine reality.

The Gita teaches that true devotion requires constant remembrance, worship, and an understanding of the divine presence in all aspects of life. Through unwavering devotion, one can attain the divine and experience the blissful union with the Supreme.

Although everyone can try to become a devotee of the Divine, Lord Krishna provides insights into the prerequisites for becoming His true devotee:

1. Faith and Surrender:

   > Give up all varieties of religion and just surrender unto Me. I shall deliver you from all sinful reactions. Do not fear. (8.66)

He assures that those who surrender to Him with complete trust and let go of all other conceptions of religion will be freed from the reactions of their past sinful actions.

2. Pure Intention:

   > Fix your mind on Me, be devoted to Me, offer service to Me, bow down to Me, and you shall certainly reach Me. I promise you because you are very dear to Me. (18.65)

He encourages individuals to fix their minds on Him, offer service, and show reverence, with the assurance that those who are dear to Him will certainly attain Him.

3. Love and Devotion:

   > To those who are constantly devoted and who meditate on Me with love, I give the understanding by which they can come to Me. (10.10)

Lord Krishna highlights the significance of love and devotion in the path of becoming His devotee. He states that those who have unwavering love for Him and meditate on Him with devotion will be blessed with the understanding that leads them to Him.

4. Self-control and Discipline:

   But those who, out of envy, disregard these teachings and do not follow them regularly, are to be considered bereft of all knowledge, befooled, and doomed to ignorance and bondage. (3.32)

He emphasizes the importance of self-control and discipline in the spiritual journey. He mentions that those who disregard His teachings and do not follow them regularly are lacking in knowledge, deluded, and bound by ignorance.

5. Study of Scriptures and Guidance:

   Just try to learn the truth by approaching a spiritual master. Inquire from him submissively and render service unto him. The self-realized souls can impart knowledge unto you because they have seen the truth." (4.34)

The above verses highlight the prerequisites to be a devotee of Lord Krishna. They include having faith, surrendering to Him, cultivating love and devotion, practicing self-control and discipline, and seeking guidance from a spiritual teacher. By fulfilling these prerequisites, one can embark on the path of devotion and attain the divine grace of Lord Krishna.

There are numerous verses that highlight the benefits of being a devotee of Lord Krishna:

1. Protection and Guidance:

   And to those who are constantly devoted and who worship Me with love, I give the understanding by which they can come to Me. (10.10)

He provides guidance and understanding to those who are devoted to Him with unwavering love. As devotees worship and seek Him, He bestows them with the knowledge and wisdom that leads them closer to Him.

2. Freedom from Material Bondage:

> Abandoning all duties, take refuge in Me alone. I will liberate you from all sins. Do not grieve. (18.66)

By taking refuge in Lord Krishna, surrendering to Him completely, and abandoning selfish desires, one can attain liberation from the bondage of material existence and the cycle of birth and death. He promises to free His devotees from the consequences of their past sins.

3. Inner Peace and Contentment:

> One who is not envious but is a kind friend to all living entities, who does not think himself a proprietor, who is free from false ego and equal in both happiness and distress, who is always satisfied and engaged in devotional service with determination, such a person is very dear to Me. (12.13-14)

Lord Krishna explains that a true devotee, who possesses qualities such as kindness, non-possessiveness, humility, equanimity, contentment, and determination in devotional service, holds a special place in His heart. Such a devotee experiences inner peace and contentment in both happiness and distress.

4. Eternal Bliss and Union with the Divine:

> To those who are constantly devoted and who meditate on Me with love, I give the understanding by which they can come to Me. Out of compassion for them, I, dwelling in their hearts, destroy with the shining lamp of knowledge the darkness born of ignorance. (10.10-11)

He dwells within the hearts of His devotees, dispelling the darkness of ignorance and bestowing them with divine knowledge. This union with the divine brings eternal bliss and liberation.

Devotion to Lord Krishna brings immense blessings and leads one towards spiritual growth and fulfillment.

Lord Krishna has given additional prerequisites for becoming a true devotee and indeed emphasizes the importance of meditation and mind control to support the thesis that one needs to have practiced meditation with yoga and controlled the mind before becoming a true devotee:

1. Control of the Mind:

> For him who has conquered the mind, the mind is the best of friends; but for one who has failed to do so, his mind will remain the greatest enemy. (6.6)

Lord Krishna highlights the significance of controlling the mind. A devotee needs to have mastery over the mind to establish a harmonious connection with the divine. Without mind control, the mind can become an obstacle on the path of devotion.

2. Yoga as a Means of Control:

> For one whose mind is unbridled, self-realization is difficult to attain. But the self-controlled and disciplined mind

> is perfectly united with the Supreme Self. (6.36)

Lord Krishna states that self-realization is challenging for those with an uncontrolled mind. However, the one who practices self-control and discipline can attain perfect union with the Supreme Self. Yoga, which includes practices like meditation, helps in attaining this control over the mind.

3. The Practice of Meditation:

> **Having made the mind one-pointed, with singleness of concentration, restraining all the senses, one should focus on the heart and meditate on Me.** (9.22)

One needs to practice meditation to make the mind one-pointed and only then can concentrate on the divine alone. By restraining the senses and focusing on the heart, the devotee can meditate on the Divine.

4. Yoga as a Means of Devotion:

> And of all yogis, the one with great faith who always abides in Me, thinks of Me within himself, and renders transcendental loving service to Me – he is the most intimately united with Me in yoga and is the highest of all. (6.47)

A true yogi is a true devotee of the Lord and among all yogis, the one who has great faith, constantly thinks of Him within, and renders loving service to Him is the most intimately united with Him. Such a devotee, through the practice of yoga, attains the highest state of union with the divine.

Gita teaches that meditation with yoga and mind control are essential prerequisites for becoming a devotee. There is an emphasize on the importance of controlling the mind, practicing self-discipline, and focusing on the divine through meditation. By developing a focused and disciplined mind through yoga, one can establish a deep connection with the divine and truly embark on the path of devotion.

Yoga in Devotion and Devotion in Yoga

With wisdom profound, Krishna imparts His lore,
Teaching devotion's essence, love's sacred core.
To be a devotee, prerequisites unfold,
With faith and surrender, one's heart to enfold.

Fixing the mind on Lord Krishna's divine face,
Offering service, with devotion's embrace.
Pure intention, a beacon to guide the way,
Love and surrender, leading to divine sway.

Control of the mind, a crucial endeavor,
For an unbridled mind, a foe to sever.
Through yoga's practice, stillness we attain,
Uniting with the divine, free from all strain.

Meditation's path, the mind we refine,
Concentration's focus, on the heart's shrine.
In devotion's fire, our spirits ignite,
With singleness of purpose, divine insight.

Becoming a devotee, with utmost grace,
Reaping benefits, the Gita does embrace.
Protection and guidance, the Lord does bestow,
Freedom from bondage, inner peace does grow.

Divine grace and blessings, a devotee gains,
Eternal bliss, where the soul forever reigns.
In this sacred dialogue, truths are unfurled,
The path of devotion, embracing the world.

Thus, the Gita's teachings, a beacon of light,
Illuminate the devotee's sacred flight.
With verses in rhythm, its wisdom resounds,
In devotion's embrace, divine union abounds.

Through devotion's flame, wisdom's grace does flow,
Bestowed upon the devotee, as seeds to sow.
With Lord's compassionate gaze, ignorance is pierced,
Divine knowledge unfolds, all doubts are cleared.

In the heart of the devotee, a lamp does shine,
Illuminating truths, both sacred and divine.
With each breath, wisdom's nectar is received,
In the embrace of grace, the devotee is relieved.

The Lord, dwelling within, guides the seeker's way,
Dispelling ignorance, as dawn conquers night's sway.
Through devotion's love, understanding takes birth,
The devotee, blessed with wisdom's infinite worth.

In moments of stillness, in prayer's sweet surrender,
The devotee's mind is graced with divine splendor.
With open heart and soul, wisdom's treasures unfold,
The devotee, in grace's embrace, securely holds.

Thus, through devotion's path, the devotee gains,
Wisdom's light, where eternal truth remains.
By Lord's divine grace, the devotee is blessed,
In wisdom's embrace, the soul finds eternal rest.

Buddhi and Discrimination

In Gita, the concept of Buddhi is associated with the faculty of discrimination, discernment, and higher intelligence. It refers to the power of the intellect to distinguish between right and wrong, to make informed decisions, and to comprehend the deeper truths of life. The Gita emphasizes the significance of Buddhi in guiding individuals towards spiritual enlightenment and righteous action.

Let us consider how Buddhi and discrimination are interconnected:

1. Intellect should be resolute:

   Those who are on this path are resolute in purpose, and their aim is one. O beloved child of the Kurus, the intelligence of those who are irresolute is many-branched. (2:41)

Individuals with a steady and determined Buddhi possess clarity of purpose, enabling them to make decisions with single-mindedness. On the other hand, those with an indecisive intellect tend to have wavering thoughts and lack the ability to discriminate effectively.

2. Buddhi steadies the mind:

   Thus, knowing oneself to be transcendental to material senses, mind, and intelligence, O mighty-armed Arjuna, one should steady the mind by deliberate spiritual intelligence [Buddhi] and so by spiritual strength conquer this

> insatiable enemy known as lust. (3:40)

This verse emphasizes the need for spiritual intelligence (Buddhi) to overcome the distractions of the material world. It suggests that by developing higher discrimination and a deep understanding of one's true nature, individuals can control their senses and conquer desires driven by lust and material attachment.

3. Intellect harnessed through devotion:

> To those who are constantly devoted and who engage in the discipline of constant remembrance, I give the understanding by which they can come to Me. (10:10)

Here, Lord Krishna implies that through unwavering devotion and continuous remembrance, individuals are blessed with an elevated understanding (Buddhi). This enhanced intelligence allows them to connect with the divine and attain spiritual union. Buddhi is not merely intellectual prowess but a higher state of consciousness that leads to spiritual enlightenment.

4. Buddhi discriminates between selfish and selfless acts:

> Those who are motivated only by desire for the fruits of action are miserable, for they are constantly anxious about the results of what they do. (18:30)

Lord Krishna encourages individuals to cultivate a discerning intellect (Buddhi) that can distinguish between actions driven by personal desires and those performed for the welfare of others. By choosing selfless actions, individuals can attain peace and liberation from the anxieties associated with the outcomes of their actions.

According to the Gita, Buddhi represents the power of discrimination and higher intelligence. It is through the development of a discerning intellect that individuals can make righteous decisions, transcend material attachments, connect with the divine, and attain spiritual enlightenment.

My Friend

Arjuna seeks guidance, his heart feeling frail.

He questions his duty, gripped by despair,
Lord Krishna imparts wisdom, showing he cares.
"Arise, O mighty warrior, stand strong and brave,
Discard this weakness, this fear you engrave.
Renounce attachment, embrace your true role,
For the eternal soul transcends life's toll.

Learn to discriminate, O Arjuna, dear friend,
Between what's eternal and what will soon end.
The body is fleeting, but the soul is divine,
In battles of righteousness, duty shall shine.

You grieve for those who may face their death,
But wise ones know life is more than mere breath.
The soul is eternal, death is just a door,
From one body to another, it will soar.

Behold, the Self is beyond birth and demise,
Like changing garments, it wears different guise.
Pain and pleasure, they come and go,
Endure them with steadfastness, let equanimity flow.

Seek knowledge, O seeker, the truth to unfold,
For wisdom breaks the chains, liberating the soul.
The senses may tempt, but control them with might,
Let reason prevail, shining wisdom's light.

Find solace in renunciation, let go of all,
Desires and attachments, watch them crumble and fall.
When the mind is steady, focused and pure,
The path to enlightenment shall surely endure.

Transcend the three gunas, the modes of the mind,
Rise above passion, ignorance, and the bind.
In Sattva, find balance, be virtuous and wise,
Free from attachment, let your actions arise.

Yoga is union, the path to attain,
Through disciplined action, the Self you'll gain.
Let go of the fruits, surrender the outcome,
Perform your duty, with devotion become.

Contemplate on the eternal, the imperishable truth,
The soul untouched by time, age, or youth.
Through self-realization, you'll find inner peace,
Attain the divine, let your worries cease.

Thus, Lord Krishna imparts his sacred word,
Guiding Arjuna, his voice like a bird.
In these verses, the essence of life is revealed,
To find true purpose, and destiny's seal.

In the Golden lotus, wisdom's light does gleam,
A sacred teaching weaves its timeless theme.
Buddhi, the intellect, its power so grand,
Discerns the path, the righteous understand.

With noble insight, discrimination's art,
Buddhi unveils the essence, sets apart
The transient veil that veils the truth divine,
Guiding seekers on their destined design.

In duty's realm, our purpose does reside,
Karma's tapestry, our actions do abide.
Each deed, a thread, woven with utmost care,
Impacting lives, creating futures fair.

Yet duty's call, not bound by mere desire,
Transcends the ego's whims, it aims higher.
For selfless action, like a radiant flame,
Ignites the soul, and drowns all sense of shame.

The Gita's teachings, like a gentle breeze,
Whisper the secrets, to souls yearning ease.
Through noble Buddhi, clarity does bloom,
Revealing paths that promise liberation soon.

So let us tread, with wisdom as our guide,

Discerning right from wrong, truth's gentle stride.

Embrace our duty, with hearts steadfast and true,

Karma's sacred dance, let love's light imbue.

Buddhi plays a crucial role in connecting the senses and mind on one side, and the soul on the other. It acts as a bridge, facilitating the interaction between these aspects of human existence.

The senses and mind, influenced by external stimuli and internal desires, often tend to pull individuals in different directions. They can be swayed by the fluctuations of pleasure and pain, attachment and aversion. However, Buddhi, the higher intellect, acts as a guiding force, enabling discernment and wise decision-making.

Buddhi helps in the discrimination between the transient and the eternal, the real and the unreal. It enables individuals to understand the impermanent nature of the sensory world and the limitations of the mind. By exercising Buddhi, one can develop the ability to make choices aligned with higher principles and spiritual truths, rather than being solely driven by sensory impulses or emotional fluctuations.

It serves as a channel for the soul's expression and guidance. The soul, in its essence, is eternal and divine, unaffected by the changes and experiences of the material world. It is the source of consciousness and inner wisdom. Buddhi acts as a medium through which the soul can manifest its inherent qualities and communicate its insights to the individual.

In the Gita Lord Krishna also explains the role of Buddhi in connection with the senses, mind, and soul:

1. Verse 2.67:

 Just as a strong wind sweeps away a boat on the water, even one of the roaming senses on which the mind focuses can carry away a man's intelligence.

It emphasizes that if the mind becomes solely fixated on the senses and their objects, it can overpower and lead astray even a person of intelligence. It is vital to control the senses through Buddhi's discernment.

2. Verse 3.42:

 The senses are superior to the gross body, and the mind is superior to the senses. But the intellect is superior to the mind, and the soul is superior to the intellect.

Here is a description of the hierarchical relationship between the senses, mind, intellect (Buddhi), and the soul. It suggests that while the senses control the physical body and the mind governs the senses, it is the intellect that holds supremacy over the mind. Additionally, it asserts that the soul is even higher and more profound than the intellect.

3. Verse 10.21:

 Of the Adityas I am Vishnu, of lights I am the radiant sun, of the Maruts I am Marici, and among the stars I am the moon.

In this verse, Lord Krishna describes various divine manifestations. It implies that the intelligence and illuminating aspect of Buddhi are reflections of the divine. Buddhi, being a higher faculty of discernment, is connected to the divine consciousness that pervades all aspects of creation.

The above verses illustrate the role of Buddhi in relation to the senses, mind, and soul. They emphasize the significance of cultivating discernment through Buddhi to overcome the influence of the senses, align with higher wisdom, and connect with the eternal soul.

When Buddhi is purified and aligned with the soul's wisdom, it becomes a powerful tool for spiritual growth and self-realization. It helps individuals recognize their true nature and purpose, guiding them on the path of righteousness and liberation.

The Gita emphasizes the need to train and refine the Buddhi through self-discipline, meditation, and contemplation. By purifying the intellect, individuals can transcend the limitations of the senses and mind, and establish a deeper connection with their innermost self, the soul.

Overcoming Mental Afflictions

In the sacred scripture of the Bhagavad Gita, specifically in Chapter 16, Lord Krishna astutely identifies three primary afflictions of the human mind. These afflictions, known as the "Three Gates to Self-destructive Hell," are Kama (desire), Krodha (anger), and Lobha (greed). Lord Krishna, in His divine wisdom, provides profound insights on overcoming these afflictions, guiding humanity towards a path of liberation and spiritual awakening.

Kama, the first affliction, refers to the intense desires and cravings that arise within the human mind. It represents the attachment to worldly pleasures and material possessions, which can lead to a state of perpetual dissatisfaction and unrest. Lord Krishna warns that succumbing to unchecked desires binds the soul to an endless cycle of suffering and delusion. To transcend Kama, one must practice self-discipline and cultivate detachment from the fruits of actions. By performing duties without attachment to results, individuals free themselves from the entanglement of desire, finding contentment in the present moment.

The second affliction, Krodha, pertains to anger or wrath. It arises from the frustration of unfulfilled desires, leading to a clouding of judgment and an inclination towards destructive behaviors. Lord Krishna cautions that anger clouds the intellect and hinders one's ability to discern right from wrong. Overcoming Krodha involves developing the virtue of forgiveness and maintaining emotional equanimity. By practicing patience and compassion, one can pacify the flames of anger, fostering a peaceful and harmonious inner state.

The third affliction, Lobha, signifies greed or avarice. It arises from an insatiable desire for accumulation and possessiveness, often leading to unethical actions and harm to others. Lord Krishna emphasizes that the insatiable appetite for more material wealth can lead to a downward spiral of spiritual degradation. To conquer Lobha, one must cultivate a sense of contentment and practice selfless giving. By embracing a spirit of generosity and detachment from material possessions, individuals can break free from the clutches of greed and experience true spiritual abundance.

In Chapter 3, Verse 37 of the Gita, Lord Krishna speaks about the entwinement of these three afflictions, stating:

> Desire and anger are born of the mode of passion; they are all-devouring, all sinful. Know them to be the enemies in this world.

To overcome these afflictions, Lord Krishna provides valuable guidance in Chapter 2, Verse 70, urging individuals to rise above these destructive tendencies:

> A person who is not disturbed by the incessant flow of desires—that enter like rivers into the ocean, which is ever being filled but is always still—can alone achieve peace, and not the person who strives to satisfy such desires.

Lord Krishna, illuminates the three gates to self-destructive Hell - Kama, Krodha, and Lobha. By practicing self-discipline, cultivating detachment, embracing forgiveness, practicing patience, and nurturing a spirit of generosity, individuals can overcome these afflictions and embark on a journey of self-realization and spiritual elevation. Lord Krishna's teachings in the Bhagavad Gita continue to serve as a timeless guide, offering profound insights into navigating the complexities of the human mind and attaining spiritual liberation.

Overcoming the three mental afflictions

In the realm of the mind, three afflictions reside,
Kama, Krodha, Lobha - in darkness they hide,
Born of desire, passion's fiery embrace,
They weave their illusions, a treacherous chase.

Kama, the first, desires uncontrolled,
A thirst for pleasures, a tale so old,
Chained to cravings, seeking endless gain,
Lost in the mirage, true peace they can't attain.

Krodha, the second, anger's burning flame,
A fury unleashed, virtue it maims,
Distorting reason, clouding the sight,
Leaving a trail of destruction in its might.

Lobha, the third, my greedy clutch,
Grasping and hoarding, never too much,
Infinite wants, insatiable thirst,
Trapped in possessions, their hearts do burst.

But fear not, for there's a way to mend,
To rise above these afflictions' trend,
Through self-awareness and inner grace,
Their hold on the soul, we can erase.

To conquer Kama, let detachment lead,
Perform your duties, but fruits concede,
Be content in the present's embrace,
Find joy in giving, not selfish chase.

To tame Krodha, practice patience's art,
Forgive and let go, let love impart,
Calm the storm, the tempest within,
With compassion, a new journey begin.

To overcome Lobha, seek a higher aim,
The path of selflessness to break the chain,
Share your blessings, let go of greed,
A heart unburdened, a soul freed.

With these afflictions dismantled and undone,
A radiant transformation will be spun,
A mind at peace, a soul set free,
Embracing truth and inner harmony.

With Kama, Krodha, and Lobha no more,
Life's wisdom and love will surely pour,
A joyful existence, a tranquil mind,
In unity with all, true bliss we'll find.

The Yoga of Wisdom

Gyana Yoga, also known as Jnana Yoga, is the path of knowledge and wisdom. The Gita emphasizes the pursuit of self-realization through the understanding of one's true nature and the ultimate reality.

1. Seeking True Knowledge:

   Gyana Yoga encourages individuals to seek knowledge beyond the realm of the physical world and understand the eternal truth::

   In this world, there is nothing as purifying as knowledge. For one who has attained it, their actions naturally lead to the path of liberation. (4.38)

True knowledge in a key to spiritual growth and liberation. By acquiring the right knowledge and understanding, individuals gain clarity and their actions align with the path of self-realization.

2. Discerning the Eternal and Temporary:

   Gyana Yoga teaches the discrimination between the eternal and temporary aspects of existence:

   That which is non-existent can never come into being, and that which is existent can never cease to be. That's what the seers of truth have concluded. (2.16)

This verse conveys the eternal nature of the soul and the transient nature of the physical world. Through Gyana Yoga, individuals cultivate the discernment to differentiate between the temporary material aspects of life and the eternal essence of the self.

3. Understanding the Imperishable Self:

   Gyana Yoga guides individuals to understand their true nature as the eternal, indestructible self.

   For the soul, there is neither birth nor death at any time. It is unborn, eternal, and ever existing. It is not slain when the body is slain. (2.20)

This verse emphasizes the immortal nature of the self. Through Gyana Yoga, individuals realize that their essence is beyond the physical body, untouched by birth or death, and eternally connected to the divine – the Self is immortal.

4. Renunciation of False Identifications:

   Gyana Yoga teaches the renunciation of false identifications, such as identifying oneself with the body, mind, or ego. In Chapter 13, Verse 33, Lord Krishna explains:

   The knowers of truth understand that the body is merely a field, and the one who knows this is called the knower of the field. (13.13)

True wisdom lies in recognizing that the physical body is a temporary vessel and the true self is the eternal observer. Gyana Yoga encourages individuals to detach from false identifications and realize their true nature beyond the limitations of the physical existence.

5. Attaining Liberation through Self-Knowledge:

   Gyana Yoga leads individuals to liberation through self-knowledge and realization. In Chapter 4, Verse 39, Lord Krishna affirms:

   Just as a blazing fire reduces wood to ashes, O Arjuna, so does the fire of knowledge reduce all actions to ashes. (4.39)

   True knowledge burns away the karmic reactions and attachments, leading to liberation. Through Gyana Yoga, individuals gain insights into the true nature of the self, transcending the cycle of birth and death, and attaining union with the divine.

Gyana Yoga in the Gita teaches the path of knowledge, enabling individuals to discern the eternal from the temporary, understand their true nature, and ultimately attain self-realization and liberation. It emphasizes the transformative power of wisdom in guiding one's actions and perception of the world.

In the context wisdom and Gyana Yoga, the terms liberation, self-realization, freedom, and God-realization represent distinct, yet interconnected concepts related to spiritual attainment. While these terms overlap to some extent, they also carry unique nuances:

1. Liberation (Moksha):
   Liberation, also known as moksha, refers to the ultimate freedom from the cycle of birth and death and the attainment of union with the Divine. It represents the release

from the cycle of samsara, where the soul transcends the limitations of the material world and merges with the eternal essence. Liberation is the ultimate goal in the Gita.

That which is night for all beings is the time of awakening for the self-controlled; and the time of awakening for all beings is night for the introspective sage. (2:72)

The implication is that the liberated one, having transcended the dualities of the material world, experiences eternal wakefulness and remains untouched by the cycles of day and night.

2. Self-realization (Atma-jnana):

   Self-realization, also known as atma-jnana, refers to the direct experiential understanding and recognition of one's true nature as the eternal soul or atman. It involves realizing the inherent divinity within oneself and understanding the eternal nature of the self beyond the transient physical body and mind.

   For the soul, there is neither birth nor death at any time. It is unborn, eternal, and ever existing. It is not slain when the body is slain. (2:24)

   Self-realization involves recognizing the eternal and indestructible nature of the self, beyond the limitations of the physical body.

3. Freedom (Mukti):

   Freedom, or mukti, can be understood as the state of liberation from bondage, ignorance, and the limitations of the material world. It refers to the release from the cycle of desires, attachments, and the identification with the ego. Freedom involves transcending the mind and realizing one's true nature as the eternal self.

The supreme state of freedom is attained by those who are self-controlled, who are disciplined in mind and senses, and who see the self within all creatures. (6.20)

Freedom is attained through self-control, disciplined senses, and the recognition of the presence of the self in all beings.

4. God-realization (Brahma-jnana):

   God-realization, also known as Brahma-jnana, refers to the direct experiential knowledge and realization of the divine nature of the Supreme Being, often referred to as Brahman or God. It involves the direct perception or union with the divine essence and recognizing the divine presence within oneself and all of creation.

   To those who are constantly devoted and who engage in the right ways of sacrifice, I give the understanding by which they can come to Me. (9.22)

   Sincere devotion and selfless sacrifice, individuals attain the understanding and realization of the divine presence.

While these concepts are interrelated, liberation represents the ultimate goal of transcending the material world and merging with the Divine. Self-realization focuses on recognizing one's true nature as the eternal soul. Freedom signifies release from attachments and limitations. God-realization involves the direct experience and union with the divine essence. (Refer to figure 4) These concepts collectively guide spiritual seekers on their paths towards attaining enlightenment and finding eternal union with the Divine.

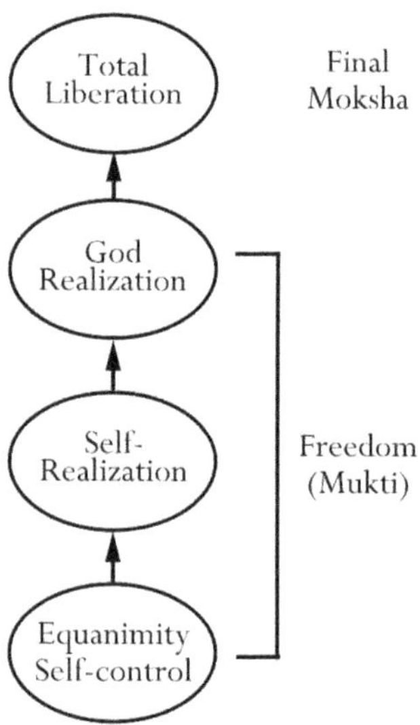

Figure 4: Stages of Moksha

Yoga of Wisdom

In yogi's rest, a wisdom profound,
A path of knowledge, where truth is found.
Jnana Yoga, the path of the wise,
Unveiling secrets behind veiled skies.

Oh, Jnana Yoga, the light of the soul,
With wisdom's flame, we become whole.
In seeking truth, our spirits soar,
In Brahman's embrace, forevermore.

With open hearts, we question and seek,
Diving deep into the realms unique.
Discerning truth from the world's disguise,
Jnana's teachings, our inner eyes.

Oh, Jnana Yoga, the light of the soul,
With wisdom's flame, we become whole.
In seeking truth, our spirits soar,
In Brahman's embrace, forevermore.

Illusions shattered, as knowledge dawns,
The transient fades, the eternal spawns.
No longer bound by the veils of maya,
In Jnana's embrace, we find our way.

Oh, JnanaYoga, the light of the soul,
With wisdom's flame, we become whole.
In seeking truth, our spirits soar,
In Brahman's embrace, forevermore.

Through introspection, our minds refine,
In silence deep, the truth shall shine.
In the realm of thoughts, we transcend,
Jnana's path, our souls shall ascend.

Oh, JnanaYoga, the light of the soul,
With wisdom's flame, we become whole.
In seeking truth, our spirits soar,
In Brahman's embrace, forevermore.

With every step, we gain clarity,
Shedding illusions, setting us free.
Self-realization, our souls ignite,
In Jnana's wisdom, we find our light.

Oh, Jnana Yoga, the light of the soul,
With wisdom's flame, we become whole.
In seeking truth, our spirits soar,
In Brahman's embrace, forevermore.

Jnana Yoga, the path of the wise,
Unveiling truth beneath the skies.
In knowledge's embrace, we find our way,
Forever grateful, we humbly pray.

Oh, Jnana Yoga, the light of the soul,
With wisdom's flame, we become whole.
In seeking truth, our spirits soar,
In Brahman's embrace, forevermore.

Epilogue

It is my hope that after reading this book, you will be inspired to utilize the Gita as a guide in your daily life.

I've demonstrated how the teachings encapsulated in many of the verses of the Gita can be applied in diverse esoteric as well as material subjects. They are of great help to navigate the minefields of a householder's journey in this world.

It is up to you to apply the teachings to deal with mundane, yet serious problems that defy logical or emotional solution, that appear in one's daily life while dealing with our needs, desire and duties.

May peace be with you!

More On The Bhagavad Gita

The Bhagavad Gita Reference Guide

The Gita has inspired and influenced Western thought since the first translation over two hundred years ago. Poets, philosophers, thinkers, and scientists have attested to its wisdom and life-changing impact.
It is the most translated Indian spiritual classic.
In this guide, the following useful reference material has been included:

- An introduction and analysis of the English translations of the Gita
- A few verses from 25 translations are provided for the reader's own comparison
- Traditional Gita Dhyanam (meditations) and Gita Mahatmyam (chants in praise of the Gita)
- The Gita Chalisa - forty selected verses traditionally considered the core teachings of the Gita
- The Gitartha Samgraha of Yamunacharya
- The ten key verses from the Advaita perspective
- The eighteen verse summary from Kashmiri Shaivism
- The epithets used for Lord Krishna and Arjuna
- A complete translation of the Gita from Swami Swarupananda
- A detailed bibliography of English translations

More Books By Rudra Shivananda

Transformed By The Presence

An illuminating chronicle of the author's journey from a spiritual seeker in a quest for immortality to a yogic practitioner guided towards Self-Realization and then flowing into an awakening to serve humanity as one's larger self through the role of a spiritual teacher. He takes us from his childhood in the British colony of Hong Kong to the eclectic mystic movements in California and the mystery shrouded spiritual realm of India, on this path of self-actualization.
The highlights of the Rudra Shivananda's accounts are the enlightening experiences he shares of his spiritual Master, the unique Himalayan Grandmaster, Yogiraj SatGurunath Siddhanath. These surreal experiences correspond to his transformational breakthroughs in higher consciousness that lead to a satisfying, joyful and meaningful life.
Rudra also shares with the reader the many different spiritual paths that he explored in his journey before meeting his Master. His insights into these spiritual disciplines are helpful to the seekers and practitioners who are still unsure of their life paths.
As a spiritual teacher himself, Rudra offers guidance on the many issues that may effect those sincere students who have shared their questions and doubts with him over the years.

Practical Nada Yoga For Self Realization

The timeless discipline of Nada Yoga has been given a renewed interpretation based on the practical experiences of the author. Rudra Shivananda provides his insights as well as practical guidance in successfully engaging on this spiritual path that leads to higher states of consciousness and to Self-Realization.

Nada is the term given to the subtle inner sounds in our deepest awareness of the cosmic Hum of the Universal Matrix. In various cultures, it has been praised as the "Music of the Spheres," the Shabda, the Sound of Creation, or the voice of the Divine: The Universal unstruck sound we seek. The vibration guides us to our core - Rudra Shivananda helps the reader to navigate the theoretical and practical aspects of reconnecting with our superconscious states.

Howling From The High Heavens

Rudra Shivananda is a well-known teacher (Acharya) of Kriya Yoga who is established in living a spiritual life in the material world. He shares his insights and experiences in a thought-provoking and impactful way through the medium of poetic verses and art forms. His purpose is to point the way to Self-Realization from various perspectives gained during his own amazing journey. He strives to move us beyond our comfortable boundaries to broader and more profound vistas of reality.

Living A Spiritual Life In A Material World

Seekers on the path of Self-Realization are soon trapped by the many pitfalls along the journey. Spiritual practices should develop the wisdom mind and lead the soul to one's True Nature or Spirit, but interacting with the demands and desires of the material world often causes the strengthening of the ego instead. When the practitioner tries to dissociate from the material world, apathy and depression results. In order to balance the spiritual life within the matrix of materiality, it is useful for the practitioner to develop within a model that encompasses both facets. This book provides the reader with inspiration and guidance along the path to navigate the treacherous waters along the river of your soul journey towards the source of Self.

In Light Of Kriya Yoga

Suitable for all those interested in expanding their awareness and how to live their lives joyfully. The author speaks from his experiential realization and connects current events with ancient teachings as well as applying parables to lives' dilemmas. He gives thought provoking and unique interpretations on topics such as: Living spiritually in a material world; do you need a Guru? liberation; Self-Realization; karma; dharma; samadhi; devotion and grace; how to develop concentration and meditation; why do good people do bad things? plus many other mysteries of spirituality. An inspirational and trustworthy companion for all those seeking to raise their consciousness to ever higher levels.

Practical Mantra Yoga

In modern times, the use of mantras has become popularized, but their reputed powers have been waning due to the proliferation of 'fast-food' mentality among those eager to grasp at results. The author, Rudra Shivananda, has tapped into the traditional mantra programs through his yogic lineage of the Siddhanath Parampara. He has re-introduced an effective graded program of three levels for attaining higher consciousness through the discipline of Mantra Yoga, one of the true and tried spiritual paths for Self-Realization.

The three levels for this practical mantra program consist of mind transformation, unity consciousness and Self-Realization. Each level is described in detail and the appropriate mantras introduced.

Breathe Better Live Longer

Hundreds of scientific studies have shown that the use of breathing techniques can help treat difficult health problems such as depression, anxiety, asthma, high blood pressure and gastrointestinal maladies.This book is a wellness program that will be helpful for preventing many health problems among young people and to heal many of the problems affecting older people.

The techniques in this program were chosen because they will show rapid if not immediate results with the investment of a short duration of practice.

Books By Rudra Shivananda

Chakra selfHealing by the Power of Om

Yoga of Purification and Transformation

Surya Yoga - Healing by Solar Power

Breathe Like Your Life Depends On It

In Light of Kriya Yoga

Healing Postures of the 18 Siddhas

Insight and Guidance for Spiritual Seekers

Practical Mantra Yoga

Breathe Better Live Longer

Superconsciousness By Practical Nada Yoga

Living A Spiritual Life In A Material World

Howling From The High Heavens

website: www.rudrashivananda.com
blog: www.sanatanamitra.com
www.youtube.com/user/KriyaNath Yogi

About the Author

Rudra Shivananda, a disciple of the Himalayan GrandMaster Yogiraj Gurunath Siddhanath, is dedicated to the service of humanity through the furthering of human awareness and spiritual evolution. He teaches that the only lasting way to bring happiness into one's life is by a consistent practice of awareness and transformation. He has developed healing programs utilizing the energy centers [Chakras] and Prana Energy techniques through breath.

Rudra Shivananda is committed to spreading the message of his Master: "Earth Peace through Self Peace". He teaches this message of World and Individual Peace through the practice of Kriya Yoga. As a student and teacher of yoga for more than 50 years, he is trained as an Acharya or Spiritual Preceptor in the Indian Nath Tradition, closely associated with the Siddha tradition. He lives in the San Francisco Bay area, and has given initiations and workshops in USA, Ireland, England, Japan, Spain, Brazil, Russia, Singapore, Malaysia, Hong Kong, India, Australia, Canada and Estonia.

www.ingramcontent.com/pod-product-compliance
Lightning Source LLC
Chambersburg PA
CBHW040407110426
42812CB00011B/2475

* 9 7 8 1 9 3 1 8 3 3 6 5 3 *